LAOS

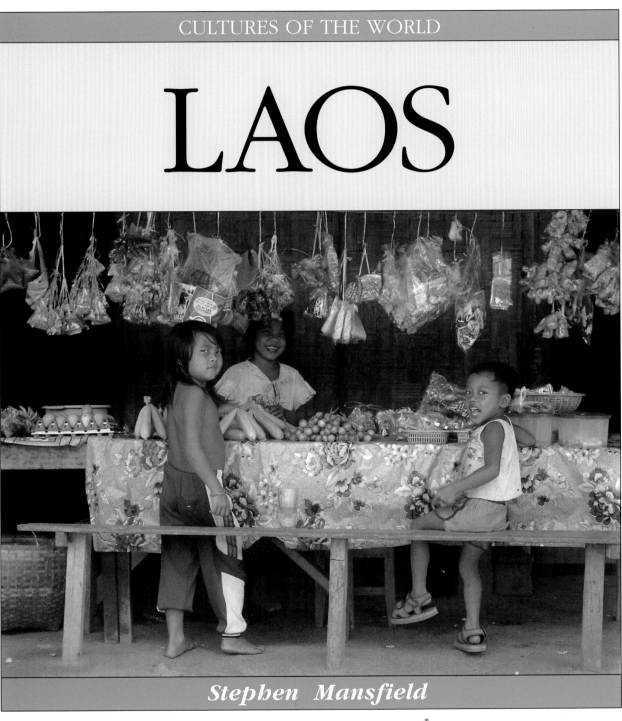

Stephen Mansfield

MARSHALL CAVENDISH
New York • London • Sydney

959.4

Reference Edition published 1999 by
Marshall Cavendish Corporation
99 White Plains Road
Tarrytown
New York 10591

© Times Editions Pte Ltd 1998

Originated and designed by
Times Books International, an imprint of
Times Editions Pte Ltd

Printed in Singapore

Library of Congress Cataloging-in-Publication Data:
Mansfield, Stephen.
    Laos / Stephen Mansfield.
      p. cm.—(Cultures of the World)
    Includes bibliographical references and index.
    Summary: Introduces the geography, history, religious
beliefs, government, and people of Laos.
      ISBN 0-7614-0689-1
      1. Laos—Juvenile literature. [1. Laos.] I. Title.
II. Series.
DS555.3.M37   1998
959.4—dc21   97–16568
                     CIP
                      AC

INTRODUCTION

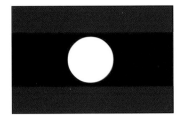

FOR MILLENNIA, landlocked Laos has sat at the intersection of two great, influential civilizations, India and China. Besides absorbing their customs and beliefs, Laos—as a small but vital part of Southeast Asia—has often been caught in the crossfire between more powerful rival states.

Today, its location could be its biggest advantage as change and economic development arrive in the area, altering the ancient rhythms of life along the Mekong River. After centuries of wars, isolation, and economic stagnation, Laos may finally be at the helm of its own destiny.

Variously described as the "forgotten land" and Southeast Asia's last "lost world," the Lao, their culture, and their land remain largely unknown to the outside world. This book will attempt to set the record straight by taking you on a journey through the lifestyles and customs of the country. It will introduce you to the many faces of the Lao people and familiarize you with one of the least known countries in Southeast Asia.

CONTENTS

Boys with their pet cockerel.

CONTENTS

Handicrafts for sale at a souvenir shop in Louang Phrabang.

WITHDRAWN

GEOGRAPHY

LAOS IS THE ONLY COUNTRY in Southeast Asia, a subcontinent consisting of more water than land, that is completely landlocked. It is the least populated country in the region and, with a landmass of only 91,430 square miles (236,800 square km), one of its smallest. Laos' diverse frontiers, however, give the impression of a country that extends far and wide.

The country is bordered to the north by the Chinese province of Yunnan, to the northeast by Vietnam, to the northwest by Burma (Myanmar), to the west by Thailand, and to the south by Cambodia. Laos is dominated by the mountains of the north and east and the great Mekong River and its tributaries. The high plateau of Xiang Khoang and the rolling Bolovens Plateau are the country's other main geographical features.

Laos has no railway system and air transport is still limited and costly. The Mekong remains the country's main highway, although steady improvements to its network of roads are now taking place.

Opposite: **Limestone hills near the northern town of Vang Vieng.**

Left: **Because of its moderate altitude, Xiang Khoang enjoys a comfortable year-round climate that is cooler than the lowland regions.**

7

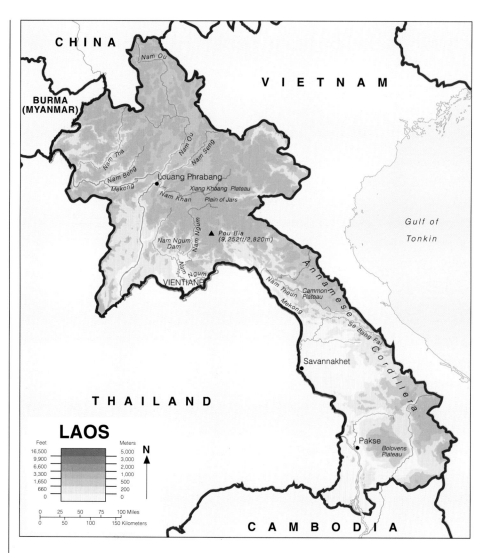

Laos is roughly 600 miles (966 km) long and 330 miles (531 km) at its widest point in the far northwest. In the narrowest part of the southern panhandle it is only 100 miles (161 km) wide, tightly walled in by the land bulges of Thailand and Cambodia. Military and colonial history has determined these borders, and in the process, the Lao have been denied access to the sea.

THE FLOOD PLAINS

With about 70% of Laos covered with rugged mountains and forested hills, the river plains and shallow valleys that can be cultivated are essential to the nation's food production.

During the rainy season the Mekong River carries great quantities of fertile silt, contributing to the region's agricultural wealth. The annual flooding of the river and its tributaries during the monsoon season assures enough sustained moisture for wet-rice cultivation. The combination of

tropical heat and the rich topsoil deposited by the river have turned these flood plains into intensely fertile areas in which to grow rice, the staple food of the Lao. Providing there are no disastrous crop failures, the flood plains can supply the entire country's rice needs.

The rivers are also an important source of fish protein. The generosity of these plains and the proximity of the life-giving Mekong account for the fact that the majority of Lao live on or near the plains, and most of Laos' key cities are located there.

The Lao have come to rely on the age-old seasonal patterns of flooding that have enriched their farms. However, in recent years the thoughtless logging of forests located on mountain slopes, particularly in the north, has caused water levels to change, resulting in excess flooding that has threatened the precious crops and livelihoods of the lowland Lao farmers.

Laos has about 1 1/2 million acres (600,000 hectares) of rice fields. The flood plains also enable the Lao to grow wheat, corn, millet, sugarcane, sundry varieties of fruit and vegetables, rubber, and cotton.

The Plain of Jars. Archeologists are still arguing about the original purpose of the jars. Whether they were rice stores, wine vats, or burial urns remains unanswered.

THE PLATEAUS

The only other level land of any sort, apart from the flood plains, is on the mountain plateaus. The largest, the Xiang Khoang Plateau, is located in the northern province of Xiang Khoang. This vast area of rolling hills and grassland reaches an average altitude of about 4,250 feet (1,295 m). Laos' highest peak, 9,252-feet (2,820-m) high Pou Bia, rises at the plateau's southern edge. The soil here is poor, yielding few crops.

The central part of the plateau, an area of extensive grassland that supports an occasional tree, is better known as the Plain of Jars. The name comes from the 300 or more stone vessels that are scattered over the plain. The jars are roughly 2,000 years old, weigh 4,000–6,000 pounds (1,800–2,700 kg) and measure between 1 and 8 feet (0.3 and 2.4 m) in height and 3 feet (0.9 m) in diameter.

The Cammon Plateau is a beautiful area of limestone hills, rivers, jungle-smothered gorges, and underground grottoes located between the Annamese Cordillera and the Mekong. The larger Bolovens Plateau lies in the southeast corner of the country's southern panhandle. A cooler altitude, plentiful rain, and fertile earth make the Bolovens Plateau, along

with the lowland plains, one of the most productive agricultural areas in Laos. Besides rice, fruits like pineapples, durians, and peaches, all kinds of vegetables, and tobacco are cultivated on the plateau. During the French colonial period the area was well known for its rubber and coffee production. Decades of war and neglect have left much of this region in ruins, but in recent years coffee production has become an important export for the country. The rubber plantations, however, continue to languish.

THE ANNAMESE CORDILLERA

The Annamese Cordillera, or Annam Highlands, a spur of the Himalayas that run from Tibet to Vietnam, is Indochina's main north-south divide. The chain runs almost the entire length of Laos. The rugged northern mountains and hills form a series of steep, sharp, parallel folds and ridges where rivers run through deep gorges. These mountains rise from 5,000 to almost 10,000 feet (1,524–3,048 m). The chain begins in the northwest of Laos and levels out in the southeast, dividing the watersheds of the region's eastern and southern flowing rivers.

The Annamese Cordillera has always been a major barrier to both movement and communication, as well as invasion. Even now, only a handful of passes cross the range.

THE MIGHTY MEKONG

The Mekong is one of the 12 great rivers of the world and the longest waterway in Southeast Asia. It flows 2,800 miles (4,500 km) through six countries. Beginning at its source in the highlands of Tibet, it passes through Burma, Laos, Thailand, and Cambodia before flowing into Vietnam's Mekong Delta and out to the South China Sea.

Of all the Mekong countries, Laos occupies the longest stretch of the river. The Mekong and its tributaries drain the country and provide a much needed source of fish, and its narrow flood plains enrich its agriculture. Its waters carry tankers and barges, and the ferries, house-boats, pirogues, and sampans that transport people and freight along the length of the country.

Only a little over half of the Lao section of the Mekong is navigable all year. Some of the northern stretches of the river, where there are rapids in the wet months and sharp, exposed rocks during the dry, can only be navigated by flat-bottomed boats for about six months of the year.

The Mekong enters Lao life through a narrow, 125-mile (200 km) gorge that slices through rugged mountains along the country's border with Burma. A little farther east, the river widens as it is joined by the Nam Khan, one of its largest tributaries. It then continues its course past Louang Phrabang, Vientiane, and onward to the southern cities of Savannakhet and Pakse. The river is only navigable as far as the Khone Falls, near the Cambodian border, where a massive natural barrier of rocks and rapids form a series of thundering cascades.

NAM NGUM DAM

The Nam Ngum Dam was opened in 1971 with the help of funds and expertise supplied by the United Nations and the United States. The dam is the first project of its kind to have been built on the Mekong. Located north of Vientiane, the dam controls flooding along the Mekong and its tributaries. Its power plant generates electricity for domestic use, but also enough to export to neighboring Thailand, supplying a good third of Laos' foreign earnings.

The Lao are very proud of the dam. Pictures of Nam Ngum and its lake are featured on postcards and tourist brochures. The lake is dotted with dozens of small islands. Valuable trees that were overlooked before the valley was flooded are now logged by frogmen using underwater chain saws.

The Nam Ngum Dam. Thailand buys some 90% of the power generated at Nam Ngum.

The Khouang-Sy water-falls, about 18 miles (29 km) south of Louang Phrabang, has been turned into a popular public spot.

CLIMATE

Depending upon the altitude, latitude, and the monsoon, temperatures are generally tropical to subtropical in Laos. The rainy season runs from May to October. The temperatures at this time are in the high 80°F (30°C) and above.

In mountainous regions like Xiang Khoang, temperatures can drop to freezing in December and January. The hottest months are March and April when temperatures soar into the high 90s (high 30°C). The coolest months are November to February, the first part of the dry season.

The level of the Mekong drops dramatically at this time, revealing little islands and sandbanks that are submerged for the rest of the year. These are eagerly appropriated by the Lao and turned into attractive kitchen gardens for the cultivation of tomatoes, beans, pumpkins, and other vegetables.

Rainfall varies considerably throughout Laos. The mountainous northern province of Louang Phrabang receives an average of about 50 inches (127 cm) of rain annually compared to the Bolovens Plateau in the south, which averages 100 inches (254 cm).

Many cultural events are connected with the seasons and climate. For example, the Rocket Festival, or *Boun Bang Fay*, in May sees the launching of giant, homemade rockets into the heavens in the hope of releasing a deluge of rain. And the end of the harvest season is a popular time for weddings.

FLORA AND FAUNA

One of Laos' greatest assets is its forests. About half the country is covered in various species of tropical and subtropical trees. Deciduous trees and hardwood forests are found on the slopes of mountains and rainforest vegetation in jungle areas. In the north there are mixed forests with large stands of evergreens, oak, and pine, while in the cultivated lowlands of the south, mango and palm trees are common. On large plateaus like the Plain of Jars, grassy savanna prevails.

Much of this green heritage is being threatened by illegal logging and by the shifting cultivation, or slash-and-burn agriculture, practiced by many of the hill tribes in Laos. Before any planting can take place, this harmful method of farming requires large tracks of land to be set on fire and then cleared with axes and hoes. When the soil's nutrients are exhausted, the farmers simply move on to another piece of land, leaving the abandoned fields to grow back to scrubland.

Water buffaloes are a common sight in Laos. Like elephants, they can only effectively work in the mornings when the temperature is cooler. They are mainly used to pull plows and carts.

15

Many varieties of animals, including some rare species, live in the mountains and jungles of Laos. These include tigers, leopards, rhinoceroses, lemurs, gibbons, several kinds of deer, wild pigs, barking deer, crocodiles, cobras, kraits, and a wide variety of birdlife, such as eagles, bulbuls, hornbills, pheasants, and hawks. Water buffaloes and elephants are trained as working animals. Elephants are used to haul large tree trunks from the forests down to rivers and roads. Traditionally, elephants were used to transport soldiers and supplies in war time. Even as recently as the Indochinese wars, elephants were used by the French, American, and communist troops as carriers. In the more remote areas of Laos, chickens, pigs, and even buffaloes are still offered in sacrifices to the gods, spirits, and ancestors of the village.

Every year, several tons of endangered species are smuggled out of the country in a growing, and increasingly profitable, illegal trade in protected wildlife.

Laos may no longer be the Land of a Million Elephants, but elephants remain strong symbols in Laos. White elephants were once associated with royalty. They are still revered as symbols of good fortune and as protectors of the land.

A RARE CATFISH

Chicken sacrifices can be seen aboard fishing boats every April in an annual ritual offering to Chao Mae Paa Beuk, a female spirit who is believed to protect the *paa beuk* ("PAH buk"), a species of giant Mekong catfish. Measuring between 7 and 10 feet (2–3 m) in length and weighing as much as 670 pounds (300 kg), the *paa beuk* is the world's largest freshwater fish.

The richest fishing grounds for *paa beuk* are found on the northern stretch of the Mekong near Ban Houayxay The fish are caught in April and May when the river level is low and the fish are making their way to Lake Tali in Yunnan province in China, to spawn. This is when the ceremony that includes the chicken sacrifice is held. The ritual takes place between Lao and Thai fishermen, who take turns to cast the large fishing nets required to catch these royal fish.

The flesh of the *paa beuk* is much prized by gourmets. But because the fish are in danger of extinction, the number of fish taken from the river is limited to 50 or 60 a year.

THE CITIES

By Southeast Asian standards, Vientiane, with a population of about half a million, is a small capital. King Setthathirat founded the capital at the strategically well-placed site of Vieng Chan in 1563, in order to protect his kingdom against invasion. A former Buddhist center, the capital was laid to waste by the Thais in 1826 and left to the mercy of the jungle for several decades before the French took control of the country.

The city is now the driving force behind the government's new economic reforms. The Friendship Bridge, completed in 1994, connects the Thai town of Nong Khai with Nalaeng, a Lao river port 10 miles (16 km) southeast of Vientiane, providing a further spur to economic change and development.

The three main urban centers aside from Vientiane are Savannakhet, Louang Phrabang, and Pakse. Savannakhet lies near the Thai border and is an important trading post.

HISTORY

THE GEOGRAPHICAL POSITION OF LAOS has always been central to its fate. Surrounded by stronger, more ambitious nations, the country has been constrained by the Annamese Cordillera to the east and the Mekong River to the west. Its history can be described as a continuous struggle to keep its political unity, and to maintain a strong national identity of its own.

Although the region of the lower Mekong Basin is known to have been inhabited by primitive tribes as long as 10,000 years ago, there are no written accounts of the early history of Laos. Legends come before historical facts. For the ethnic minorities of Laos in particular, most of whom have no written records of their own, legends are the only real way of explaining and transmitting information about their origins.

Above: **Modern-day renditions of mythical figures said to be the first male and female ancestors of the Lao.**

Opposite: **The Patuxai in Vientiane commemorates the Lao who died in wars prior to the 1975 revolution.**

ANCIENT MYTHS

Legends that explain the origin of the Lao people take many forms. The best known account tells how the first ancestor of the Lao, Khoun Borom, was sent by the King of Heaven to rule over the land. Mounted on a white elephant, Khoun Borom discovered a vine bearing two giant gourds.

When these were pierced, men, women, animals, and seeds poured out. Using these resources to establish their own domains, Khoun Borom's seven sons divided the land among themselves, founding seven Tai principalities.

A Khmer stone found near Vientiane reveals that the city may have been established in the fifth or sixth century.

EARLY MIGRATIONS

At this point historical facts and legends begin to merge. The Lao are a branch of the Tai peoples, who long before recorded history occupied a large area of Yunnan province in China.

The name "Lao" first appears in Chinese and Vietnamese annals during the shadowy period between the third and 14th centuries when the Tai peoples were migrating from Central Asia into southern China. By the eighth century, they had established the strong military kingdom of Nan Chao in Yunnan.

Even then, these Tai tribes were gradually moving toward the borders of present-day Laos, Vietnam, Thailand, and Burma. The pace of this slow, southward migration from Yunnan quickened in the 13th century with the fall of Ta-li, the capital of Nan Chao, to the armies of Kublai Khan.

LAND OF A MILLION ELEPHANTS

The recorded history of Laos begins a hundred years after the fall of Nan Chao with the birth of Fa Ngum in 1316. Fa Ngum grew up in exile with his father, a Lao prince, at the court of Angkor in Cambodia. It was here that he studied and later adopted the Buddhist faith and married a Khmer princess.

With the help of the Cambodian king Fa Ngum succeeded in uniting the Lao kingdom of Cham Pasak in the south, Xiang Khoang in the northeast, and the kingdom of Muong Swa and its royal city, Louang

Phrabang, in the north. This brilliant warrior was also a champion of Buddhism, a creed that he made the state religion.

Under his rule, the borders of the country were extended to include large parts of southwest Yunnan, eastern Siam (Thailand), the Korat Plateau, and most of present-day Laos. Fa Ngum named the kingdom Lane Xang, the Land of a Million Elephants.

The work of Fa Ngum was continued by his son, Samsenthai (1373–1416), and other rulers who followed. The capital was transferred from Louang Phrabang to Vieng Chan, as Vientiane was then known, by King Setthathirat in 1563. A number of palaces, libraries, and Buddhist temples and monuments were built at this time.

After Setthathirat's death in 1571, Burma invaded the kingdom, which then collapsed into anarchy. After the arrival of King Souligna Vongsa (1637–94), a long period of peace and security followed, heralding Lane Xang's Golden Age. Ruling for 57 years, the longest reign of any Lao monarch, Souligna Vongsa further expanded his kingdom's territory and power.

At the height of its power, Lane Xang also achieved fame as a center of Buddhist learning, attracting monks and scholars from Siam, Burma, and Cambodia. It was at this time that the first Europeans visited the country.

An elephant mural at Wat Ipeng in Vientiane.

The temple of That Luang was damaged repeatedly by invading Burmese and Siamese armies after the death of Souligna Vongsa. In the early 20th century, it was restored and reconstructed by the French.

THE DECLINE OF LANE XANG

The decline of Lane Xang began with Souligna Vongsa's death. In the absence of a male heir to the throne, the country soon split into three separate kingdoms: Louang Phrabang in the north, Vieng Chan in the center, and Cham Pasak to the south. Each established its own alliances

with powerful neighboring states. This stressed the divisions between the three kingdoms and prevented them from reuniting into a strong single kingdom. Between the 18th and late 19th centuries, these much weakened states were riven by invasions from Burma, Siam, and Annam (Vietnam), and their own internal quarrels and instability.

Anger over foreign intervention and frustration with the nation's decline came to violence in 1826 when King Chao Anou of Vieng Chan suddenly rebelled against Siamese influence. The rebellion was short-lived; the Siamese armies captured and razed Vientiane, forcefully resettling thousands of inhabitants on the west bank of the Mekong.

With Vientiane now a vassal of Siam, and gangs of Chinese marauders terrorizing the north and east, the country was ready to fall into the hands of colonial powers.

FRENCH RULE

France's early interest in Laos centered on finding a river passage to southern China. French efforts to navigate the Mekong and open up a trade route halted when Khone Falls in the south proved impassable. The French then shifted their interest to exploiting the country's raw materials for their industries at home and their other colonies in Indochina.

By the end of the 19th century the French had succeeded in setting up a protectorate in Laos and had united its much reduced borders into a single union again. Although the French did little to develop the country and often neglected to involve the Lao in the decision-making process, their rule was, by and large, a mild one.

It was under the French, however, that the seeds of an independence movement were first sown.

The French saw Laos as a useful buffer state between the two expanding empires of France and Britain. Under the new colonial masters, the capital reverted to Vieng Chan, which the French dubbed Vientiane, and the country became known for the first time as Laos.

The tomb of the great French naturalist and explorer, Henri Mouhot, near Louang Phrabang. While exploring the tributaries of the Mekong River, Mouhot discovered the ruins of Angkor in Cambodia in 1858. He died from jungle fever in 1861.

Bomb craters caused by American B-52s on bombing missions to the Plain of Jars during the Vietnam War.

LAOS AND THE SUPERPOWERS

During World War II Laos was occupied by the Japanese. The inability of the French to defend Laos and the eventual surrender of the Japanese in 1945 gave great encouragement to the newly-formed Lao Issara (Free Laos Movement). Although the French were to prevail for a few more years, full sovereignty was eventually granted to Laos in 1954.

National unity continued to elude the country, however, as it sunk into internal division and involvement in the political problems of its neighbors, particularly Vietnam. In the period known as the Cold War, Laos became the focus of global interest. The spread of communism and the conflicting ideologies of the rival superpowers—the Soviet Union, the United States and China—soon transformed Indochina into a battlefield.

With different political factions vying for power, the country soon disintegrated into civil war and a rapid succession of coups. Laos was split three ways: between the neutralists, who officially represented the royalist government, right-wing American sympathizers, and the Pathet Lao. The Pathet Lao was a left-wing resistance movement strongly affiliated with the North Vietnamese communists.

As the conflict in Vietnam escalated, Vientiane became a center for American undercover operations in the region. North Vietnam's main supply route, the Ho Chi Minh Trail, ran along Laos' eastern border. The trail, along with the Plain of Jars, a Pathet Lao stronghold, and other strategic provinces, were furiously carpet-bombed by the Americans. The United States also deployed a CIA-backed "secret army" in Laos, made up mostly of US-trained Hmong and Thai mercenaries. By the time American troops began pulling out of Vietnam in 1972, and a ceasefire was signed in Paris the following year, over three quarters of a million Lao had been forced to flee their homes because of the fighting.

The heroes of the communist struggle in Laos are remembered today in the country's Revolutionary Museum.

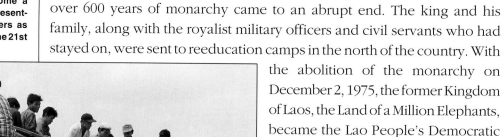

INDEPENDENCE AND BEYOND

Reconstructing their country has become a priority for Laos' present-day political leaders as they look toward the 21st century.

With the decisive takeover of the country by the Pathet Lao forces in 1975, over 600 years of monarchy came to an abrupt end. The king and his family, along with the royalist military officers and civil servants who had stayed on, were sent to reeducation camps in the north of the country. With the abolition of the monarchy on December 2, 1975, the former Kingdom of Laos, the Land of a Million Elephants, became the Lao People's Democratic Republic.

The new government immediately faced a number of major social and economic problems. The end of aid from the United States coincided with an economic blockade by Thailand. Hundreds of thousands of displaced refugees had to be resettled.

To make matters worse, most of the country's qualified administrators, doctors, and engineers fled the country. They were soon joined by large numbers of businessmen, traders, mechanics, and artisans. In the 10 years following the revolution, over 300,000 Lao left the country as refugees.

Agricultural collectives were set up, religion socialized, and property belonging to members of the old

RECYCLING THE PAST

For the Lao who live in Xiang Khoang, even wars have their uses. Materials left over from the last Indochina war have been turned into helpful commodities. A brisk trade in recycled war scrap has grown over the years, with flare casings, bombshells, and pieces of airplane fuselages being collected and hoarded and then sold to scrap metal merchants to be melted down and resold for commercial use.

War debris that is not sold is often stored by residents in the space under their stilted houses and then removed when a use can be found for it. There are many examples of the resourceful uses to which the Lao have put this war scrap.

Many shell casings serve as fences, cattle troughs, water vessels, pillars to support houses or barns, and as planters for growing vegetables. In one village, a B-52 shell casing hangs from a frame at the side of the road, serving as a fire-bell. Passersby may also notice bomb craters that have been pressed into harmless service as fish and duck ponds. Lotuses can often be seen blooming on the surface of the water.

regime confiscated. The farming cooperatives, which were not only unpopular but economically unmanageable, were abolished in 1979 and replaced with a more moderate form of market socialism. Russian aid to Laos ended in the late 1980s.

A steady improvement in relations with non-Socialist countries resulted in the resumption of international aid to Laos. Many Buddhist ceremonies and festivals associated with the country's traditional culture have been revived and peace, stability, and even the prospect of moderate prosperity, may have returned at last to Laos.

GOVERNMENT

SINCE THE REVOLUTION, the official name of the country has been the Lao People's Democratic Republic (Sathalanalat Pasathipatai Pasason Lao). This is often shortened for purposes of business and correspondence to Lao PDR, or more simply, the LPDR. In French, it is the RDP.

The French designation, Laos, is still commonly used by foreigners and in most books and articles about the country. The Lao themselves refer to their own country as Pathet Lao. "Pathet" means country, or land. It is becoming common now among Western residents and diplomats to refer to the country as Lao, dropping the "s," which the French introduced. The Lao people are sometimes called Laotians, but this too is being dropped in favor of the Lao.

Laos is divided into 16 provinces (khwaeng, "kwar-ENG"). Each province, including Vientiane, which is an independent prefecture, is divided into districts (muang, "MOO-ang") that are further divided into two or more subdistricts or cantons (tasseng, "TAH-sen") made up of villages (baan, "BAN").

Opposite: **The Unknown Soldiers' Memorial was built to remember the Pathet Lao who died during the communist struggle in the 1960s and early 1970s.**

Left: **The elephant and the national flag—symbols of today's modern Lao state.**

ADMINISTERING THE COUNTRY

The central governing body in Laos is the Lao People's Revolutionary Party (LPRP). The LPRP is directed by the party congress. The congress meets every four to five years to elect new party leaders.

The National Assembly (formerly the Supreme People's Assembly) is the nation's main legislative branch. Members of the assembly are elected by Lao citizens for five-year terms. Since the revolution the assembly's membership has varied between 40 and 45 representatives. Its main purpose is to meet once a year to hear, discuss, and approve statements by the prime minister.

The executive government is nominally headed by the prime minister, who is appointed by the president of the republic, with the approval of the National Assembly. The president is also in charge of appointing provincial governors and mayors. The National Assembly is also responsible for electing and replacing the president of the republic.

Other important government organs are the Central Bureau of the Central Committee, a Permanent Secretariat, and the Council of Government, which consists of 14 ministries.

THE CONSTITUTION

Following the 1975 revolution, the government officially became Marxist-Leninist in its political philosophy. Communist rule existed without a written constitution for the first 15 years.

The first independent constitution of Laos was endorsed in mid-1991. Internal reforms took place and several members of the old guard retired. At the same time, it was announced that the state motto, "Peace, Independence, Unity, and Socialism," would henceforth be "Peace, Independence, Democracy, Unity, and Prosperity."

A judicial system was set up, with the People's Supreme Court as its highest appeal.

FOREIGN RELATIONS

Relations between Laos and its neighbors have improved considerably in recent years. Violent border clashes with Thailand in the late 1980s have been resolved. Visits by members of the Thai royal family and the opening of the joint Thai-Lao Friendship Bridge in 1994 have gone a long way to ensuring that landlocked Laos has both an ally and an open door for trade and commerce along its long western frontier.

Relations with China have also thawed in the years following a state visit to Beijing by then President Kaysone Phomvihan in 1991. Laos is the only country in Indochina to have maintained relations with the United States since the revolution, even though the latter has never offered aid or financial reparation for the damage it caused to the country during the Vietnam War. Ties with the United States have strengthened since Laos agreed to cooperate over two key issues—the narcotics trade in the Lao section of the Golden Triangle and the search for the remains of American military personnel "missing in action" in the mountains and jungles of Laos.

With the end of Soviet aid and the withdrawal of most of its technical advisers and diplomatic staff, Laos has turned more and more toward Thailand, the West, and Japan, its largest aid donor, for economic assistance. Trading partners Australia, France, and Germany also provide aid. Bilateral relations with Vietnam have remained cordial, but Laos' dependence on its old ally has weakened as it has developed relations with other countries in the region and farther afield. The withdrawal of some 50,000 Vietnamese troops from Laos in 1987 and the death in 1992 of President Kaysone Phomvihan, who was half-Vietnamese, have led to a further severing of historical links between the two countries.

The Lao government is hoping that in the future it will be able to benefit from its role as a bridge between its powerful neighbors, without being overwhelmed by them.

With the introduction of pro-capitalist economic reforms in the early 1990s, the old state emblem, the Russian hammer and sickle and the Vietnamese star, was quietly removed from all official documents and replaced by the silhouette of That Luang, Vientiane's foremost Buddhist temple.

A billboard for the United Nations Children's Fund (UNICEF) in downtown Vientiane. UNICEF is one of several United Nations organizations active in the country.

ECONOMY

LAOS IS ONE OF THE POOREST COUNTRIES in the world. A large foreign debt, a lack of skilled workers, and a per capita income of just over US$300 a year paint a bleak picture. The quality of life, however, particularly at the social and cultural level, gives a more positive impression.

Most of the country's self-reliant villages produce sufficient amounts of food to live on and to exchange with neighboring villages. The system of agricultural collectives introduced by the communists proved unpopular and was soon abolished. Most farmers now own their own land.

By 1979 it was clear that Marxist economic policies were not working. With the country tottering on the edge of bankruptcy, the government introduced sweeping reforms. The New Economic Mechanism, or Open Door Policy, was launched in 1986. By the mid-1990s, capitalism had started to take firm root and the effects were beginning to show, especially in the cities.

Above: **Lao currency. In recent years, the kip has maintained its value well after years of instability.**

Opposite: **Making rice cakes. Food processing is one of Laos' most common small-scale enterprises.**

The government began by loosening restrictions on private enterprise. State-owned businesses and factories that were not profitable have been sold. Inflation has dropped from a runaway 80% in 1989 to below 7%. The nation's gross domestic product has averaged a healthy 7% since 1992. The Lao unit of currency, the kip, has remained stable.

In this more progressive economic climate, and with the country about to join the ASEAN group of nations, foreign investors are looking more favorably at Laos. Foreign aid is also pouring into the country now, helping, at least for the time being, to balance its loan deficits.

AGRICULTURE

Almost 80% of the population are engaged in agriculture. Less than 10% of the country's total land area, however, is exploited for agricultural use. Rice is the main food staple of the Lao. It is grown by both lowland wet-rice farmers and highland dry-rice, hill tribe cultivators. Output has steadily increased in recent years, but crops are still heavily dependent on weather conditions. Floods, droughts, a long cold spell, or a plague of rats can have devastating effects on the rural economy.

Other important lowland crops include corn, wheat, cassava, soy beans, fruits and vegetables, and cotton. Major cash crops produced in the mountain areas are tea, opium, coffee, tobacco, and cardamoms. Another important activity in recent years has been livestock breeding, especially cattle and pigs.

Lao rivers provide a large and reliable yield of fish. Experiments in fish breeding are now taking place in the massive reservoir formed when the

Nam Ngum Dam was built. If these projects are successful, Laos will be able to export freshwater fish to Thailand in the near future.

MINERALS

The remoteness of deposits made mining uneconomical until now, but with improvements in the transportation network, more of Laos' mineral wealth is beginning to be extracted. The country's rich mineral resources will be a great asset in the future.

Laos has large deposits of lignite, iron ore, copper, lead, zinc, coal, gypsum, phosphorus, and manganese. Many of the areas in which these deposits are located have yet to be surveyed. Other largely untapped resources include gemstones and reserves of gold. A number of foreign companies are engaged in surveying for oil, and others have been granted mining and exploration rights.

Planting rice seedlings is labor-intensive work. Laos produces over a million tons (910,000 metric tonnes) of rice every year.

Laos' abundant forests include valuable wood such as rosewood, mahogany, ironwood, teak, and pine. Despite strict government-imposed quotas to conserve forest resources, illegal logging has been difficult to control.

Erosion and deforestation of mountain slopes prevents water retention. When it rains, water rushes down the slopes, flooding valleys and rice plains.

FORESTRY

About half the country is still covered in primary forest. Almost a quarter of this total consists of teak and other valuable, high-quality hardwoods. Over half the country's export earnings come from logging. Successive bans on excessive logging and a government reforestation program have failed to compensate for the destruction of Lao forests. Over 1,000 square miles (2,590 square km) of mountain forest disappear every year.

Corruption, a lack of trained forest rangers, and porous borders make it relatively easy to smuggle wood out of the country. The activities of illegal loggers, many of whom are Thai, continue to reduce the country's canopy of green.

Efforts by the government to limit the devastation caused by shifting cultivators who destroy large tracts of forest each year when land is cleared for planting have met with more success. Underskilled and undermanned, Laos is now calling for international assistance to implement its forestry program.

THE BATTERY OF SOUTHEAST ASIA

Along with timber, wood processing, and minerals, revenues earned from the export of hydroelectricity to Thailand is one of the country's largest foreign exchange earners. At present, most of this comes from the Nam Ngum Dam north of Vientiane and the Xeset Dam in southern Laos. These account for over US$20 million a year in export earnings. The country's hydroelectric capacity is estimated to be almost 20,000 megawatts.

A power station on the Nam Dong currently supplies the city of Louang Phrabang with electricity. With the resurfacing of the northern stretch of Route 13, Louang Phrabang will be linked to the Vientiane valley power grid. Another project at Nam Theun, near Thakhek, plans to export all the electricity generated to energy-hungry Thailand. If approved by all the other nations that make up the influential Mekong Committee, more projects to exploit the rich potential of the river and its tributaries are likely in the future.

Although Laos' hydro-electric potential is enormous, the rural population continues to rely mostly on fuelwood for its energy. Almost 90% of the country's total energy consumption comes from wood.

A market stall selling China-made toys.

INDUSTRY AND TRADE

Although the state has expanded the private sector in the hope of producing and manufacturing more goods for domestic use, Laos continues to depend heavily on imports. The majority of these imported goods are financed by foreign aid.

The country's leading export earners include electricity, timber, wood processing, the receipts earned from overflight rights, and the garment industry. Laos' manufacturing base, however, remains tiny.

The main areas in which companies operate are tobacco and food processing, soft drinks, leather, paper, sawmills, handicrafts, textiles, pottery, brick and cement production, and other small-scale enterprises. Thanks to a steady flow of foreign investment coming into the country, more joint manufacturing ventures are probable. With a population of under five million, however, Laos is unlikely to become an industrial giant in the foreseeable future.

Laos' biggest trading partner by far is Thailand. Much trade is also conducted with France, Japan, and China. Imports, consisting mainly of oil and other petroleum products, machinery and motor vehicles, food products, and medicines, outweigh exports significantly.

BRIDGE OF NO RETURN

Nothing symbolizes the economic opening up of the country better than the Friendship Bridge. The bridge, which was officially opened on April 8, 1994, is the country's link with the outside world.

The bridge connects Vientiane with the Thai town of Nong Khai, and is the first such construction to span the Mekong. The 0.7-mile-long (1.1 km) bridge was financed with US$30 million of Australian aid. The opening of the bridge was attended by a number of important people, including the Thai and Australian prime ministers, the Lao president, and King Bhumibol of Thailand. The bridge is a key link in the development of overland routes that will eventually connect Laos to Singapore in the south and Beijing to the north. The bridge has also been designed to accommodate a railway line if required. It is possible in the future that rail links will be built in Laos to connect northern Thailand and Yunnan province in China with Hanoi in northern Vietnam.

The Friendship Bridge. The Lao government is proceeding slowly before it accepts a Thai proposal to build another bridge farther south. While happy with the Friendship Bridge, Laos is concerned about the negative effects of unrestricted access to the country, such as crime, traffic, and environmental problems. Despite the changes taking place, Laos remains a deeply conservative country.

TRANSPORTATION

One of the major keys to the country's economic development is the improvement and extension of its network of roads. There are over 9,000 miles (14,490 km) of roads in Laos, including national highways, provincial roads, local roads, and Routes Coloniales, constructed by the French. Many are paved with asphalt, others are just gravel tracks. Route 13, running from Louang Phrabang in the north to Vientiane, Savannakhet, Pakse, and the Cambodian border in the south, is the country's longest single road. Other routes run east from this main artery and cross over the high mountain passes of the Annamese Cordillera into Vietnam.

Many road building and improvement projects are being financed by outside bodies like the Asian Development Bank, the World Bank, and the Swedish government. Travel by road within Laos can be slow, even hazardous, during the rainy season. When completed, the improved road system will help to transport people and goods more efficiently and safely.

TOURISM

Tourists have only begun to travel to Laos in recent years. In the 1960s few visitors traveled far beyond Vientiane and the old royal city of Louang Phrabang. The war in Indochina led to a complete suspension of tourism. The country finally opened its doors to visitors in 1989, but then only conditionally.

Since then tourists have started to trickle in. Even now the number of foreign visitors to Laos is estimated to be no more than about 16,000 a year. Outside of the main cities, hotels, restaurants, and other facilities are limited. The government is worried that too many visitors will have a negative impact on its culture and way of life. It hopes to promote what it calls "cultural tourism," rather than mass tourism. Whatever happens, the country's rich history and culture, its colonial buildings and Buddhist temples, magnificent scenery, and attractive hill tribes, are certain to attract the curiosity of more visitors in the future.

A bright hotel signboard welcomes potential guests. A relaxation of government restrictions on the movement of foreigners has helped increase tourist traffic.

THE LAO

THE ESTIMATED POPULATION OF LAOS in 1996 was 4.5 million. In comparison with other Asian countries, Laos, with a population density of only 49 inhabitants per square mile (19 per square km), is sparsely inhabited. The government is, therefore, encouraging population growth. Improvements in health and sanitation have helped to reduce the high infant mortality rate, and children now make up a large proportion of the population. The population is forecast to double by the year 2014. The average life expectancy remains low at 50.

Over two-thirds of the population live in the rural provinces, although a steady urbanization is taking place. The most populated provinces are Savannakhet (692,000), Vientiane municipality (503,000), and Cham Pasak (490,000). One of the country's greatest problems is the lack of an integrated population. Historically, Southeast Asia has been a melting pot for different races, cultures, and religions. Laos has the highest number of minorities in the region. The Lao Lum, the country's earliest settlers, are the national race. The Lao Lum are about half the population.

There are four main ethnolinguistic groups. The Lao Lum are the country's lowlanders; the Lao Tai dwell in the upland valleys; the Lao Theung occupy mountain slopes and river valleys; and the Lao Soung, the country's highland dwellers, generally live at altitudes of over 3,000 feet (914 m). There are over 60 different ethnic minorities in Laos.

Above: **A villager in Louang Phrabang province with an old hand-made flintlock rifle.**

Opposite: **A mother and daughter at the market.**

THE LAO LUM

The Lao Lum are a subgroup of the Tai peoples who once occupied Yunnan province in southern China. From the Chinese they learned about wet-rice farming and the martial arts. This helped them to settle and gain mastery of the Mekong flood plains and to force other groups up into the higher areas. Today most city and town residents are Lao Lum.

The Lao Lum, who refer to themselves simply as Lao, are the country's dominant racial group. They are the architects of most of the nation's main traditions, institutions, and many of its customs. The language of the Lao Lum is close to that of the Thais, especially those living in the northern province of Thailand called Esan.

The official language of the country is the Lao spoken by these lowland people. The state religion, Theravada Buddhism, is also the faith of the Lao Lum.

THE LAO TAI

The Lao Tai, who mostly inhabit the mountain valleys of northern Laos, are closely related to the Lao Lum. They subsist as farmers, growing wet rice, millet, corn, sweet potatoes and beans, as well as dry rice and wheat on mountain slopes.

Unlike the Lao Lum, the Lao Tai have generally maintained their animist beliefs. Strong believers in spirits, they will go to great lengths to appease the more malevolent ones. The Lao Tai include groups like the Black Tai and Red Tai (names taken from the color of their clothing), and the Northern Tai.

Although Western clothes are becoming popular among the young, many Lao Lum women still wear embroidered, wrap-around skirts called *pha sin* ("PAH sing"). These are worn with silk or cotton blouses. The centerpiece of a Lao Lum woman's clothing is her finely decorated silver belt. On special occasions like weddings or festivals, a silk shawl called a *pha biang* ("PAH bee-ang") (see photo) is also worn.

THE LAO THEUNG

The Lao Theung are believed to be the original inhabitants of Laos. They are an Austro-Indonesian tribe and are sometimes referred to as the Indonesian group. About one-quarter of the population belongs to the Lao Theung, the second largest group in the country.

Their language belongs to the Mon-Khmer group. Large numbers of Lao Theung are found in the north and east of the country and on the Bolovens Plateau. Traditionally the Lao Theung have lived a seminomadic existence as slash-and-burn farmers and hunters. Many have now settled on the land and cultivate crops like rice, corn, cotton, tobacco, coffee, and tea.

The Lao Theung often live together as extended families in large wooden longhouses built on piles. The buildings are made from bamboo, timber, and woven cane. They are spacious and usually have high roofs. Some Lao Theung have adopted Buddhism like the Lao Lum. Others have remained animists.

Their place in Lao society has often been lower than other groups. They were known in former times as Kha (slaves). Members of Lao Theung tribes like the Khamu, Lamet, and La worked as court servants before the revolution. Even now, many Lao Theung are found working in poorly paid manual jobs for the wealthier lowland Lao.

THE LAO SOUNG

The Lao Soung, who represent about 17% of the population, are the most recent arrivals in Laos. Their migrations from China occurred only in the last 250 years. They are the most ethnically distinct of all the groups. They are known in Laos as the Chinese group. The main tribes belonging to this group are the Hmong, Man, Akha, Yao, Mien, Ho, and Lolo.

The Lao Soung belong to the Tibeto-Burman language family. The Lao Soung are practicing animists. Elements of ancestor worship, Buddhism, and even Confucianism surface in their religious rituals, ceremonies, and feasts.

These highlanders consider themselves superior to the lowland Lao. This has often led to differences between the two groups. Tensions also exist between the various Lao Soung groups themselves. The Lao Soung are a fiercely independent people. They dislike being restricted by government policies and consider themselves free to cross over into other countries at will. Large numbers of Lao Soung are found in Burma, Vietnam, China, and Thailand.

Many of the Lao Soung are shifting cultivators, but there are also settled communities. Villagers grow corn, cassava, mountain rice, tapioca, sugarcane, and root vegetables like yams. They also breed animals, including water buffaloes and horses.

A Hmong woman. Some 50,000 Hmong now live in the United States, after leaving Laos following the 1975 revolution.

HILL TRIBE FASHIONS

Lao hill tribe dress, particularly that worn by women, is useful in distinguishing one ethnic group from another. In some cases, the name of a tribe may even be decided by their color and design preferences. In the case of the Hmong, for example, the main groups are described as Black, Blue, White, and Stripped Hmong, according to the color and type of the women's dresses.

Styles vary greatly with each group. The Hmong are known for embroidered designs, strips of colorful applique, and their dyed and pleated skirts. The Yao are noted for their baggy trousers, long tunics, bright red ruffs, and the pom-poms worn by their children. The Lanten, a little known minority, are striking for their white leggings, indigo trousers, and the women's custom of shaving their eyebrows. The Ahka (picture) are characterized by close-fitting headdresses decorated with coins, bright metal disks, shells, and beads.

Silver is regarded by the hill tribes as a source of wealth, like money in the bank. Silver pendants, chains, rings, bracelets, and breastplates are dazzling when worn against black, red, and indigo cloth. Old silver coins are used by some groups as earrings and necklaces and to decorate the borders of headdresses and the hems of skirts. Many of these are old French colonial coins, others come from China and Thailand. Old Burmese and Indian rupee coins from the days of the British empire can also occasionally be seen. Silver buttons beaten from coins are also an important hill tribe decoration.

It is not surprising that the strong visual impact of hill tribe fashions have begun to influence Western designers.

The Lao Soung are known for their excellent manual skills. Many of the tribes produce tools, as well as silver ornaments and textiles. The high ground occupied by the Hmong is also perfect for the growing of poppies, from which opium is made. This has been an embarrassment to the Lao government, who are now trying to stop the production of this cash crop.

OTHER COMMUNITIES

The Chinese are one of the largest foreign communities in Laos. The majority of Chinese residents live in the cities of Vientiane and Savannakhet. They work as restaurant and repair shop owners, and as retailers and wholesalers. Many shops, hotels, and cinemas in Laos are owned by ethnic Chinese.

Another important minority are the Vietnamese. The French and later the North Vietnamese government encouraged their settlement. They follow similar trades to the Chinese, but tend to live in border and rural areas. Their number has decreased in recent years. There are a small number of Khmers (Cambodians) living in the southern province of Cham Pasak. They mainly work in the fields of trade and transportation.

With improved relations between Thailand and Laos, an increasing number of Thais are taking up temporary residence as business people and as workers in the education and aid sectors. A small number of Indians, Pakistanis, and Bangladeshis have made Vientiane their home. They are mostly shopkeepers, tailors, and tradesmen. Some of them can also be seen selling fabrics and cloth every day at the large morning market.

These days, a small but growing number of Europeans, Australians, Americans, and Japanese can be found living and working in Laos. Many of those who are not running businesses work for organizations like the United Nations and the World Health Organization (WHO), or for one of the many nongovernmental organizations like the Red Cross.

A Vietnamese-Lao monk. Until recently, large numbers of Vietnamese lived in Laos. They still represent a significant minority.

LIFESTYLE

THE COMMUNIST REVOLUTION IN LAOS tried to replace loyalty toward family, village, and pagoda with loyalty to the state. Centuries of foreign incursions, the French colonial period, and the new political doctrines of the 20th century have had relatively little impact on rural lifestyles and ways of thinking, however. Even now, most rural Lao have little contact with the world beyond their own village. Their lifestyles are largely prescribed by the seasonal routines of an agricultural way of life. Radical change and upheaval are contrary to the Lao character. As one Lao proverb puts it, "Let the dog bark, let the caravan pass by."

The Lao are an individualistic people, who generally dislike extremes of behavior. Politeness, patience, moderation in speech, modesty, self-restraint, and respect for elders are important aspects of the Lao character that have influenced their way of life. The Buddhist idea that people should follow a "Middle Way," is reflected in people's distaste for conflict, their willingness to compromise.

The ideals of modern socialist states, with their five-year plans and goals of national unity and construction, have left little impression on the largely self-sufficient Lao village. For most lowland Lao, the predictability of the seasons and a generally reliable rice harvest have ensured a fairly comfortable and conservative existence in keeping with Buddhist teachings.

Capitalism, with the promise it offers of acquiring a new radio or motorbike, is likely to have a far greater impact in the long run on the life of the average Lao than any political theory ever could.

Above and opposite: **As Laos seeks to revolutionize its economy, changes to the lifestyles of its people are almost inevitable.**

A young girl helps her mother with the chores. Lao families are closely-knit, with everyone pitching in to share the workload.

THE RURAL CALENDAR

Annual patterns of work and life for most rural families are divided into two seasons: rainy and dry. The coming of the southwest monsoon rains in May signals the busy planting season. Most of the work is done by hand. There are few tractors or other agricultural machines. Oxen are still used to plow the fields.

Rice, once it has sprouted, is prepared in bundles and transplanted into corner sections of fields for a few days before it is planted in prepared paddies. At this time many villages hold ceremonies to propitiate the guardian spirit, or *phi* ("PEE"), of the rice fields. This period of intensive work lasts for about 100 days. The important task of weeding the paddies continues until the October harvest.

During the growing season, men fish and hunt, repair things around the village, and make simple farming implements. The women concentrate on growing vegetables, cooking, and looking after the house. If they have any free time they may do a little weaving. The care of livestock, like water buffaloes, is entrusted to children. This is also the period for the Vassa, the Buddhist Lent. Monks retreat into their monasteries for the remainder of the rainy season. With the dry season more intensive activity returns. There are ceremonies and celebrations to accompany the end of the harvesting, threshing, winnowing, and storing of the rice.

Except for the occasional bad year, crops are regular and consistent. This fact perhaps explains the conservatism and general satisfaction felt by most rural Lao with their way of life. For the dry farmers of mountain regions like those in northern Laos, it is different. Variations in the weather and poorer soil give them less reason to feel secure.

Villages are usually built near a source of water. In the highlands, however, someone has to fetch water from rivers and valleys every day and carry it up to the mountain villages.

A French-style house in Vientiane serves as a reminder of colonial rule, which ended in 1953.

URBAN LIFE

Laos is the least urbanized country in Indochina. There are no cities to compare in size or mood with the likes of Phnom Penh or Hanoi. The capital, Vientiane, is the only Lao settlement that remotely resembles a city, although Savannakhet is a developed commercial center and Louang Phrabang an important cultural one.

Part of Vientiane's charm has always been that it has remained a provincial backwater. Its tree-lined avenues, crumbling old French villas, and riverside bars and cafés are reminders of a different age. In recent years some of that charm has vanished with greater prosperity, the arrival of foreign investors and aid workers, and the influence of nearby Thailand. For better or worse, discos, brand name goods, Western clothes, and Thai television and pop music are all now part of the Vientiane scene.

EDUCATION

Traditionally the education system in Laos was run by monks. Classes were held in the courtyard of the local pagoda. With the arrival of the French, secular schools were introduced and the French language taught. Some schools in Laos are still attached to monasteries and pagodas, although the teachers are no longer monks.

With the creation of the LPDR, the Lao People's Revolutionary Party began a policy aimed at providing a basic education for all children and eradicating illiteracy among the adult population. Although literacy levels remain low in comparison with neighboring countries like Vietnam and Thailand, government statistics suggest that the policy is working.

Primary education in Laos begins at the age of 6. Secondary education starts at 11 and lasts for six years. There are over 7,000 schools in Laos.

War disrupted the education of much of the population. These young Lao, however, are making up for the lost opportunities of their elders.

There is only one university in the country, Sisavangvong University, located in Vientiane, and several regional technical colleges. During the 1970s and 1980s, many students were sent to the Soviet Union or Vietnam for higher education.

Education is compulsory, but not always possible to enforce, especially in remote rural areas or among seminomadic hill tribes. In 1991 enrollment at primary schools included about 59% of children in the primary age-group. Secondary enrollment, on the other hand, included just 15% of that age group. More males than females were in school. Teachers' pay remains low and funds for textbooks and other materials are often in short supply.

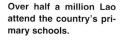

Over half a million Lao attend the country's primary schools.

HEALTH

Despite great strides in building up the economy in the last few years, the country remains desperately poor. This is reflected in its standards of health and medical care.

Public health has steadily improved in the cities, however. A major hospital was built with Soviet help in the 1980s. At present there are eight central hospitals, 16 provincial units, and 115 district hospitals, served by over 9,000 doctors, assistant doctors, nurses, and other staff.

The health structure was greatly affected by the departure of many of the country's doctors after the 1975 takeover by the Pathet Lao, and remains weak. Despite assistance from foreign organizations and much effort on the part of the government, there is still a chronic lack of basic medicine, essential equipment, and experienced personnel.

In the countryside, a widespread belief in the supernatural origins of illness has hindered some health programs, especially the immunization of children.

The Louang Phrabang hospital. Laos' infant mortality rate, at 193 per 1,000 live births, is one of the highest in the world. Malnutrition is common, and almost half the population suffers from either malaria or one form of intestinal disease.

Women grinding grain.
Females make up a vital
part of Laos' labor force.

WOMEN

The division of labor between the sexes in rural areas is almost as rigid now as it was generations ago. Men plow the fields, hunt, fish, build boats, fell trees, make basic tools, repair fences, and pursue other similar tasks.

Women's work, if anything, is even harder. They are responsible for the running of the household and bringing up the children. In addition, they are expected to cook, clean, spin and weave, carry wood, look after the kitchen garden, and be responsible for the backbreaking task of carrying and fetching water. They are also obliged to hull rice by pounding it in a large mortar with a heavy pestle. Women play an important part in economic activities outside the home as well. Most of the bartering and selling of produce in the markets is conducted by women.

Many women fought alongside men in the country's struggles for independence. Although their level of education is higher than before the revolution in 1975, few real measures have been taken to improve the traditionally subordinate position of women in Lao society. In sharp contrast to Vietnam, where women have been encouraged to develop leadership skills, women have played a relatively minor role in the history of Laos. Politics remains an almost exclusive male preserve with very few women occupying senior positions in the government.

MARRIAGE

Arranged marriages are no longer common in Laos. Although the choice of a life partner is usually a personal matter, the heads of both families are consulted in advance of the wedding. The steps leading up to marriage are complex. A formal request for the bride is usually made in the presence of a village elder or monk.

Both families usually consult an astrologer to make sure that the couple's birthdays and fates are well-matched. It is the parents who decide when the couple will marry, where they will live, and the sum to be paid as a bride-price (*kin dong*, "keen DONG"). This is delivered to the bride's father on the day before the wedding. On the same day the groom's family will turn up at the bride's house with gifts of food, betel nuts, and other offerings.

Couples are married by village elders or a local monk in a simple Buddhist ceremony that requires no exchange of rings. Traditional Lao dress is worn by both the bride and groom, a distinctive Lao ceremony called a *baci* ("BAH-see") is held, and sumptuous food served at the reception. It is thought lucky to entertain strangers during the ceremony.

For most Lao, married life began with a memorable ceremony.

Traditionally, brides were abducted by the groom's friends and relatives in a pantomime of fighting and wrangling. In the southern provinces of Pakse and Cham Pasak, the "kidnapping" of brides would take place with an elephant as the means of escape.

BIRTH AND ADULTHOOD

The naming ceremony of a newborn child is the first big event in a Lao person's life. A *baci* in which money is attached to the infant's arms, is held for family members, friends, and neighbors or, if in a village, the entire population. The size of the feast depends on the wealth of the family. A bonze (Buddhist monk) is asked to choose a name for the child, one that will depend on the astrological conditions at the time.

For a boy, the next most important ceremony is one which marks his transition from childhood to adulthood. The manhood ceremony usually takes place around the age of 13. It is a ritual involving the cutting of the boy's hair to which only close relatives are invited. In more traditional areas, boys still sometimes receive a tattoo as a symbol of manhood, which has the added value of warding off evil spirits.

DEATH

The final and most important ceremony for a Lao is the funeral. The ministrations of bonzes at funerals is mandatory and more marked than for baptism or marriage. They are involved in almost every stage of the elaborate ceremonies up to the final cremation.

After the body has been prepared, it is placed in a coffin and private family rituals are held. Expressions of grief are kept to a minimum as the Lao firmly believe that displays of sadness retard the rebirth of the spirit of the deceased into a better existence, one step closer to the final goal of *nirvana* ("ner-VAH-na").

After the family rites, the body is placed in a shelter in the garden or yard, and a series of feasts and ceremonies begins. The body is finally taken to a cremation pyre on a river bank or in a field, washed, exposed to the sky, and then cremated.

Families who cannot afford these elaborate rituals resort to a simple burial in the forest. Graves are left unmarked in such cases, and it is hoped that all trace of the burial spot will vanish as quickly as possible, otherwise the spirit of the dead person runs the risk of joining the malevolent spirits believed to harass villages and travelers in remote areas.

A funeral pyre about to be set alight.

RELIGION

THERAVADA BUDDHISM has, more than any other single force, influenced and shaped the Lao character. Theravada means Doctrine of the Elders. Its followers claim that it is a purer branch of Buddhism than the broader Mahayana, or "Great Vehicle" school. Theravada Buddhists claim that their sect keeps more strictly to the teachings of the Buddha, as set down in the Tripitaka, or Three Baskets, the Buddhist scriptures. Theravada Buddhism, sometimes known as the "Little Vehicle," is found in Sri Lanka, Thailand, Burma, Cambodia, and Laos.

Theravada Buddhism has influenced the Lao in their conduct and attitudes as well. Little emphasis is placed, for example, on the accumulation of wealth for its own sake. It is a common practice for the Lao to set aside a part of their slender funds as a donation for the upkeep of the local pagoda or monastery.

Opposite and left: **Monks are respected figures in the community. Apart from their religious and moral duties, they are often consulted about family problems and matters of general welfare. Traditionally, they also played the role of teachers and healers. Responsibility for bonzes or monks places a heavy economic burden on families, but the Lao appear happy to shoulder the cost. The presence of so many monks provides the Lao with countless opportunities to earn merit.**

ADVENT OF BUDDHISM

Fragments of Buddha statues dating back to the Khmer occupation of Laos in the eighth century have been found in the Vientiane area. Buddhism was practiced in this region as early as the 11th and 12th centuries. It was not until the arrival of Fa Ngum and the founding of the kingdom of Lane Xang though, that Buddhism as an organized system of belief took root in Laos.

Fa Ngum was known in Laos as the Great Protector of the Faith. It was Fa Ngum who carried the Phra Bang, a small golden statue of the Buddha, from the Khmer court in Cambodia. The figure was originally cast in Sri Lanka before being taken to Angkor. It is of immense importance to the Lao who regard it as the symbol of Lao Buddhism.

King Setthathirat championed the Buddhist faith in the 16th century by building many temples and monasteries. During Lane Xang's golden age, Vientiane became an important Buddhist center in Southeast Asia. Its importance was lost after many temples were destroyed by the Thais when they sacked the city at the beginning of the 19th century.

Because it is forbidden to destroy any kind of Buddha image, broken images are piled up in temples, caves, and other holy places.

Buddhism declined even further after 1975 under the communist regime. People were prohibited from giving alms to monks and the teaching of Buddhism was banned from primary schools. These days, with increasing government tolerance and support, Buddhism is undergoing a revival. Temples are again lively centers of learning and worship and many are being restored and redecorated.

THE *JATAKA* TALES

Printing was only introduced to Laos in 1957. Before that, Lao literature was written in manuscript form. Many manuscripts were engraved on palm leaves. Some of these have survived and are kept in museums or in the libraries of monasteries and temples. Some of the most interesting manuscripts are those that contain the *Jataka* tales.

The *Jataka* tales are central to Buddhist literature. This collection of stories concerns the previous *jataka* ("jah-TAK-er," incarnations or lives) of the Buddha. These former existences of the Buddha are called Bodhisattvas. The tales describe the long journey of the Buddha and his passage through the various animal states and different human conditions, to his final attainment of *nirvana*. The stories are a colorful vehicle for Hindu folklore and fables, the teaching of Buddhist ethics, satirical asides, and even humor. Fifty Lao *jataka* recounting local folk tales have been added to the original 547 tales that appear in Pali.

The stories are painted in bright, often garish colors, on the outside walls of temples and shrines. They are often painted in panels like a comic strip. The Lao enjoy the stories just as much for their entertainment value as their religious and moral aspects.

BUDDHIST TEACHINGS

Lao Buddhists try to follow the example of the Buddha, born Siddhartha Gautama, the son of a Nepalese prince who lived over 2,500 years ago in the north of India. Siddhartha's wanderings and meditations were rewarded when he attained enlightenment under a bodhi tree, after realizing the Four Noble Truths.

The first of these states that life is pain, suffering, disease, old age, and death. The second is that these are caused by desire and attachment to worldly things. The third truth is that detachment from such concerns can offer an end to suffering and the endless cycle of rebirth. The fourth truth is that in order to free oneself from these it is necessary to follow the Noble Eightfold Path.

The Eightfold Path consists of right understanding, thought, speech, action, livelihood, effort, mindfulness, and concentration. This is known as the "Middle Way." It avoids two extremes: the pursuit of happiness through either pleasure or self-inflicted pain. The ultimate goal of all Buddhists is to free themselves from the tiresome cycle of existence and rebirth known as *samsara* ("sum-SA-ra"), and enter *nirvana*. This ideal condition is often defined as "extinction of self," and can be described as a state of nothingness in which a Buddhist is finally free from suffering. In the Buddhist world view, the universe and all living forms are in a constant state of change from birth to death. After death comes rebirth, the so-called Wheel of Rebirth. According to the thoughts, deeds, and speech of one's life, there are three planes of existence to which beings can be reborn. These are the animal and ghost realms, the human plane, and the celestial one.

The Buddha's teachings are known as the *Dharma* ("dar-MER"). It is the responsibility of Buddhist monks to pass on these teachings to the people. The Buddhist clergy (the *sangha*, "sang-GHER"), the Buddha himself, and the *Dharma* are known as the Triple Gem.

Devotees perform a ritual offering.

All good Buddhists try to follow the commands of the Buddha as expressed in the Five Precepts: do not take life, do not steal, commit adultery, speak falsely, or take intoxicating drinks. Each relapse from the important Five Precepts by which the Lao try to conduct their daily lives postpones the achievement of *nirvana*, just as the accumulation of merit brings it nearer.

Monks on an alms round. The monk gives no thanks for the offerings he receives. Because gifts of this kind are a chance to acquire merit, gratitude is not expressed or expected. It is the giver, in fact, who thanks the monk for providing the chance to feed him and gain merit by the act.

ALMS GIVING

There are various ways in which Lao Buddhists can gain merit. Good deeds, acts of generosity, and respect for elders are common means to gain merit in the next life. The pagoda (*wat*, "what") is the center of village life. Merit can be earned by donating money to the local Buddhist order, helping with the cost of building a new temple, sponsoring a religious ceremony, or by paying for the ordination of a monk. Most young men will undergo a period of ordination at some stage in their lives. This is one effective way for a son to acquire merit for his family, especially his mother and sisters who, as women, cannot be ordained.

Monks depend upon the local population for most of their material needs. Pagodas are always located near population centers. Everyone has an opportunity to earn merit each morning by offering alms to monks as they file through the streets at dawn.

In Laos it is mainly women who can be seen doing this. The women place rice, vegetables, and other delicacies into the monks' bowls as they pass.

THE PAK OU CAVES

The impressive Pak Ou caves (above) are located opposite the mouth of the Nam Ou, a tributary of the Mekong, some 15 miles (24 km) north of Louang Phrabang. They are set dramatically into limestone cliffs overhanging the Mekong River. The upper cave is known as Tham Phun, the lower as Tham Thing. The two main caves are sanctuaries for thousands of Buddha images.

The caves were discovered by King Setthathirat in the 16th century. The statues, made of wood and gold, are over 300 years old. Many of them were brought here for safekeeping during periodic attacks on Louang Phrabang. The statues vary in height from just a few inches (cm) to 6 feet (2 m). Many of the statues have been carved in classic attitudes like the "Buddha Calling For Rain."

Once inhabited by monks, the caves are now believed to be the home of guardian spirits. The Pak Ou caves are sacred to the Lao, and a visit here is seen as a pilgrimage. Before the revolution the Lao king used to visit the caves every year during the *Pi Mai* festival and conduct a candle-lighting ceremony. Hundreds of people still make the trip in boats from Louang Phrabang during the festival to make offerings and light candles in the gloom of these sanctuaries.

IMAGES AND MUDRAS

Buddha images, especially statues, have survived war and destruction better than Lao temples. Unlike old bomb casings, bronze and gold Buddhas are never melted down, however ruinous their condition. Buddha images throng the insides of temples, monasteries, and sacred caves. They can be seen standing in the open along the roadside, commanding the crest of a hill, or ranged along the outside pavilions of temples.

Apart from being works of art, they are also objects of worship. Images are represented in different *mudras* ("moo-DRAHS"), or attitudes. Ancient Pali texts and Sanskrit poetry have set down certain characteristics of the Buddha that have influenced Lao artists.

The Buddha is usually represented sitting, standing, lying, or, less commonly, walking. There are about 40 *mudras*. Lao Buddhas have some unique features. These include elongated ears, a sharp, beaked nose, and surprisingly slender waists. The following are some of the most popular *mudras* used in depicting the Buddha in Laos:

The Buddha Calling for Rain In this *mudra*, the Buddha is standing with his hands pointing downwards towards the earth. This image is rarely found outside Laos.

Bhumisparcamudra ("boo-miss-PAH-cam-moo-DRAH"). Also called "Touching the Earth," or "Calling the Earth Goddess to Witness," this *mudra* depicts the Buddha's enlightenment and victory over Mara, king of the demons.

The Buddha's right hand is placed over his right knee. His fingers point to the earth.

Over half the population are practicing Buddhists. Many of the hill tribe peoples maintain a primitive belief in spirit worship and supernatural forces. Even the Buddhism practiced by people in the cities retains a uniquely Lao character, incorporating centuries-old elements of animism, Brahmanism, and ancestor worship.

A typical Lao *mudra*. The figure's right hand is reaching across his knee to touch the earth.

Dhyanamudra ("yan-AH-moo-DRAH"). A common image in which the Buddha is seen meditating. Open palms face upward, resting on his lap.

Abhayamudra ("ab-hay-YAH-moo-DRAH"). This means "Giving Protection," or "Dispelling Fear." The Buddha's right palm is usually raised in front of his chest as if holding back evil.

A sacred cave at Vang Vieng. Many Lao villages have a spirit grove where the *phi* live.

SPIRIT GROVES

If Buddhism is the official religion of the lowland Lao, animism, or spirit worship, is the dominant belief of many of the hill tribe peoples. For most Lao, there is no contradiction in observing both Theravada Buddhism and animist practices. Even for the Lao Lum, belief in *phi* (spirits), and the superstitions and rituals that surround them, happily coexists with Buddhism.

The belief in *phi* is often combined with ancestor worship. There are basically two types of spirits that the Lao pay attention to: mischievous or malign ones, and guardian spirits. Evil spirits may be spirits of the dead or spirits of place. Lao villagers and mountain dwellers are careful to avoid jungles and lonely, unexplored places at night. One widespread belief is that it is dangerous to walk on all fours in the forest. Anyone who does this runs the risk of possession by the spirit of a tiger. It is also considered inadvisable to walk along a lonely riverbank at night in case of attack by a water spirit. This would cause the person to believe he is a fish, and lengthy and costly offerings would have to be made to the spirit before he was released.

The Lao spend as much time making offerings to ensure the favors of the guardian spirits as they do to propitiating the evil ones. Rituals to Nang Prakosob, the female spirit of rice, for example, must be carefully observed if there is to be a good harvest. Most villages have two main protective spirits—the *phi wat*, guardian of the temple, and the *phi muang*, the protector of the village.

OTHER RELIGIONS

Laos' 1991 constitution guarantees freedom of religious belief. The majority of Lao, however, feel comfortable and content with their unique mixture of Buddhism and animism and show little interest in converting to other faiths.

In the aftermath of the 1975 revolution, Christian missionaries were expelled from the country. But with more religious tolerance these days, Christianity is again openly practiced, and groups like the US Bible Society are active once more.

There are an estimated 18,000 Christians in Laos. Most are found among either the French-educated Lao class that remained in the country after 1975, or among growing numbers of animist hill tribes. A large number of Christian missionaries and priests are believed to be operating in remote areas of the country, some under the umbrella of various nongovernmental organizations.

Islam, on the other hand, has had little impact on Lao life. There are about 200 Muslims living in Vientiane and Savannakhet. A small mosque in Vientiane holds services every Friday and is a meeting place and study center for the capital's Muslim population. Most Lao Muslims are of Pakistani or Bangladeshi extraction. Many of them have married Lao women, who then converted to Islam.

A French cathedral. There are four Apostolic Vicariates in Laos.

ນ.13

ມ.ຫຼວງພະບາງ

KM

LUANG PRABANG

15 KM

372

LANGUAGE

LAO, THE OFFICIAL LANGUAGE OF THE LPDR, belongs to the Tai group of languages. Tai is part of a language family that extends from Assam in India to Yunnan province in southern China. There are Tai speakers in northern parts of Vietnam, Burma, Thailand, and pockets of China such as Kwangsi and Sichuan.

Standard Lao as spoken in the region of Vientiane has become the lingua franca of all Lao, including ethnic minorities who may have their own distinct languages and dialects. The Lao spoken today is quite different from the language spoken before the revolution, especially in the Vientiane area. Many honorifics and other respectful forms of address have disappeared as the regime has tried to create a more classless society. Large population movements after the war have introduced local and regional words into the language that have become part of a common, shared vocabulary.

Opposite: **An old milestone informs travelers how much farther it is to their destination.**

Left: **A Lao television reporter and camera crew at work. A domestic television service started in December 1983, and by 1992 there were over 28,000 receivers in use.**

THE TONAL SYSTEM

Lao is a monosyllabic, tonal language. Any polysyllabic words found in Lao are mostly those borrowed from Pali and Sanskrit, ancient Indian languages. Words have also crept in from Khmer, French, English, and even Persian. Spoken Lao uses six different tones. These consist of three level tones (high, mid-range and low), one rising tone, and two falling ones. As with most languages, the pitch at which the language is spoken is not absolute and will vary from speaker to speaker.

There are 33 consonants in Lao. These fall into three groups: the low, high, and rising. Because almost all of the high and rising consonants have identical sounds, the 33 consonants actually only produce 20 distinct sounds in all. There are 28 vowel sounds in Lao. These are divided into long and short sounds. A slight change in inflection can drastically alter the

An example of the Lao script. Before 1975 there were very few printing presses in Laos. Textbooks and advanced manuals were printed in either Thai, French, or Vietnamese.

meaning of a word. The word *khaa* ("car") in the low tone, for example, can mean "crow;" in the mid tone, "price;" and "to kill" in a low, falling tone.

Although Lao grammar is surprisingly straightforward, the tonal system can, at least in the beginning, be a stumbling block to foreigners wishing to learn the language.

THE LAO SCRIPT

Like Cambodian, Thai, and Burmese, written Lao has its origins in the ancient scripts of southern India. The oldest written documents still in existence in Laos date back to the 16th century.

Lao manuscripts (*kampi*, "kem-PI") were usually engraved on palm leaves and then threaded together with cord. Sets of 20 leaves were bundled together and wrapped in cloth for safe keeping, but many have suffered from the passage of time, the tropical climate, and attacks by insects.

Other scripts have been used throughout the centuries in Laos. These include scripts for spoken Yao, for writing Pali, a Thai Neua tribal script, and a Chinese-based system used in the 16th century. Modern Lao is modeled on a script devised by the Thai King Ramkhamhaeng in 1283. Modern Lao is written from left to right. There are no spaces between words.

There were four spelling systems in use before the revolution. These have been standardized into one single phonetic script that expresses both the sound of the word and its pitch.

A trishaw passes by a building signboard.

Hand-painted propaganda boards like this are common in Vientiane.

LAO AND THAI

The Lao and Thais understand each other very well. Standard Thai is similar enough to Lao for the two to be mutually intelligible. Most of the differences that exist between the two spoken languages now stem from the French colonial period when Lao was insulated from the changes going on in the Thai language.

Lao is spoken in the north of Thailand and in its northeastern province of Esan, which was originally part of the Lao kingdom of Lane Xang. This northeastern dialect is virtually the same as Lao. Strangely, there are said to be more Lao speakers living in this region of Thailand than there are in Laos itself.

Because most of the textbooks used at college and university level were, and continue to some extent, to be in Thai, most educated Lao can understand the written script as well. Thanks to the popularity of Thai television and radio programs that are transmitted daily over the Mekong, almost all Lao can understand spoken Thai.

SIGN WRITING

A shortage of commercial printing presses and industrial stencilling facilities has meant that much advertising has traditionally been done by hand. Sign writing is still a thriving profession in Laos. It is a common sight in the streets of Vientiane to see commercial artists painstakingly working on a shop sign at the front of a shop or on the pavement outside.

Most shop signs are still hand-painted. The shopkeeper and the artist must first agree on a suitable design or motif before the work is undertaken. Sketches are then made and colors chosen. The tropical monsoon climate, with its heavy rainfall and strong sunlight, will eventually rot or blister the work, particularly if it is painted on a wooden surface. If the advertiser is happy with the design, it may be necessary for the sign writer to come back two or three years later to touch up the advertisement.

Some of the most fascinating examples of hand-painted messages combining language and imagery are the large propaganda billboards visible in cities and areas of high population density. Some of these are as much as 9 to 13 feet (3 to 4 m) in width. For large, raised messages, scaffolding may have to be erected and a team of four or five painters assigned to the work.

LANGUAGES OF THE MINORITIES

Russian linguists in the 1980s estimated that there were over 600 dialects spoken among the hill tribes of Laos. Although there are numerous local dialects, branches, and subdivisions of Tai languages, many of these are mutually intelligible to the respective groups. With the exception of one or two groups like the Yao, very few of the tribal groups have their own written script. Other important language families that exist among the hill tribes of Laos include:

TIBETO-BURMESE. The Lahu, Lisu, and Akha are examples of tribes within this group. They are mostly concentrated in the northern region of Laos.

HMONG-YAO. This important group originated in southern China and includes the Mun language of the Lanten. Groups of Hmong and Lao are found in China, Thailand, and northern Vietnam.

MON-KHMER. There are over 30 tribal groups in this language family. The best known are the Alak, Soh, and Suei, who live in the south, the Lamet from the north, and the Pai and Khamu, who can be found all over Laos.

New propaganda murals are often produced, and old ones touched up, before special events like Lao National Day, a public holiday that celebrates the 1975 revolution with street parades and speeches.

"Learning English is ABCD," proclaims this schoolboy's bag. Like much of the rest of the world, the Lao are beginning to realize the economic importance of English.

FRENCH AND ENGLISH

Until the early 1990s, French was the preferred second language of the educated Lao class, government workers, and administrators. Even now it is the country's official second language. Shop signs, restaurant menus, and some legal documents are often written in French, along with Lao translations. It is also used in the tourist industry as the French at the present time constitute the largest number of Western visitors to Laos.

PROVERBALLY YOURS

Lao, in common with other languages, contains a rich and colorful assortment of proverbs. Many reflect aspects of the national character, ways of thinking, culture, the folklore of the hill tribes, and even the geographical features of the country. The following are a small selection from the hundreds that exist in the Lao language:

When one has heard, one must listen, and when one has seen one must judge with one's heart.

Medicine can cure the bite of a poisonous snake, but nothing can master a wicked heart.

When the buffaloes fight it is the grass that suffers.

A tray full of money is not worth a mind full of knowledge.

Some are brave in the village, but cowards in the forest.

When the water level falls, the ants eat the fish. When the level rises, the fish eat the ants.

An empty pot makes a loud noise.

Do not soil the shade of a tree that has been hospitable to you.

Young Lao, like their neighbors in Vietnam and Cambodia, prefer to learn English than French. As English rapidly takes over as the principal medium of international commerce in the region, French is likely to become less and less relevant to the lives of people living in the Indochinese peninsula.

ARTS

FOR CENTURIES Laos has been the target of foreign domination and greed. Its towns and cities have been plundered and its treasures removed. Repeatedly ransacked by Thais, Chinese, and Vietnamese, and then bombed by the Americans, it is surprising that so much of the Lao cultural heritage has survived.

Although Lao culture has its roots in many nearby countries, it is recognized as distinct from its other Southeast Asian neighbors. The country has its own architecture, music, written language, handicrafts, dress, and popular customs. Decades of war, civil strife, and revolution, however, have left their mark on this fragile nation. Now that peace, security, and the prospect of modest prosperity have come to the historically contentious countries of the Mekong, a modest revival of the arts is taking place in Laos.

Opposite: **Wat Phu, near Cham Pasak, was once a Hindu temple.**

Left: **Gold-painted wooden panels at Wat Xieng Thong. The Lao have excelled at wood carving for centuries.**

LITERATURE

Many of the subjects and forms of Lao literature, like those of neighboring Thailand and Cambodia, bear the strong imprint of Indian influence. The roots of Lao literature are based on a strong oral tradition. Much of the literature that has survived consists of long epic poems and verse novels. Many of these were originally set to musical accompaniment. Stories and poems were sung or chanted by balladeers who roamed the country. The most famous work of Lao literature, an epic poem called the *Sin Xay*, was originally sung and recited.

The new writing skills that came with the arrival of Buddhism in the 14th century meant that stories gradually were written down. Classical tales

Over the centuries, the Buddha has become the subject of many stories. As a wealthy prince who lived in sixth century B.C. Nepal, he gave up his life of luxury and eventually discovered the path to enlightenment.

typically focus on love, heroic deeds, mythology, and the history of the gods. Religious literature, like the *Jataka* tales, deals with the Buddha's birth and his previous forms of existence. One popular story concerns a legend about the Buddha footprint found on Mount Phousi in Louang Phrabang. There are several spiritual and philosophical texts based on Buddhist concepts as well. Religious literature borrows many of its characters from the Indian pantheon. Prahin, or Indra, is a popular figure in classic Lao literature. Many Lao manuscripts were, unfortunately, taken to Bangkok after the Thais razed the capital in 1828.

Historical chronicles are another literary form found in Laos. Most of these were written in Pali by anonymous authors. The best known is the *Nilan Khun Borom*, the History of King Khoun Borom. Many of the popular stories and novels found in Laos are based on the Indian canon of tales called the *Panchatantra*. Adventure and the supernatural are the main ingredients of these stories.

Tales about animals who have human characteristics are popular in Laos. Some are reminiscent of *Aesop's Fables*. These are contained in several volumes of stories entitled "The Bull," "The Frogs," "The Demons," and "The Birds." Echoes of another familiar story, *Cinderella*, can be found in the Lao tale called *Pa Pul Dan*, which is all about a young girl and her selfish stepmother.

A traditionally carved manuscript box.

Dancers rehearse some of the finger movements needed to perform the Lao version of the *Ramayana*. Scenes from the *Ramayana* can be seen all over Laos. Dance dramas enact some of the favorite scenes, like the monkey god Hanuman's battles, and the abduction of Sita. Figures and scenes from the *Ramayana* are also found in the many murals and carvings of Lao temples.

THE LAO RAMAYANA

The *Ramayana*, or *Ramakien*, is an epic verse play written by the Indian poet Valmiki. The drama, which tells the story of the Indian king Rama and his wife Sita, is performed all over Southeast Asia. Its influence on the arts and culture of the region has been enormous.

The Lao version of the *Ramayana* is known as the *Pra Lak Pra Lam*. Although it follows the original story of the life of Rama and Sita, the Lao version has many original features. The action takes place not in India, but along the Mekong valley. The first 20 pages of the Lao version of the work set the scene with a description of the geography and landscape of Laos.

Subplots and local myths and folklore have been added to the original. Although the story remains basically the same, the background scenery has been changed and characters adapted in such a way that any Lao would recognize the setting and morality of the story as their own.

NAGA SYMBOLISM

Lao art and legends are full of stories and images of *naga* ("NAR-ger"). The *naga*, or *nak* ("nak"), as it is better known in Laos, is a mythical water serpent that resembles a cobra. The *naga* was an important symbol in Southeast Asia even before the advent of Buddhism or Hinduism in the region.

The *naga* is a symbol of both destruction and renewal. In Hindu-Buddhist legends, the *naga* was responsible for causing a great drought to spread over the earth after it drank all of its waters. An ancient Khmer legend relates how a king, whose domains were suffering from a terrible drought, fired rockets into the sky. Shiva was so pleased that she let the rains fall. Many of the rockets used in the May Rocket Festival are decorated to resemble *nagas*.

The Buddha is believed to have been protected by the hood of a *naga* when facing the demon Mara. *Naga* images appear all over Laos. Their mouths are always open, and their heads may look like snakes or dragons. *Naga* heads frequently support the roofs of temples. Five- or seven-headed *nagas* often guard the entrances to temples. Single *nagas*, with their bodies stretched to fantastic lengths, may decorate the balustrades of staircases leading up to hilltop temples. They are placed there to remind visitors of their symbolism as a bridge between two worlds, the earthly and spiritual. They provide a good example of the way ancient myths, legends, and folk symbolism in Laos is interwoven with orthodox Buddhism.

The prow of a racing boat designed in the form of a *naga* head.

After its construction in the 16th century, Wat Xieng Thong remained under royal patronage until the 1975 revolution swept away the monarchy.

WAT XIENG THONG

Wat Xieng Thong is the most important royal temple in Louang Phrabang. It was built in 1559 by King Setthathirat and is the only building of its kind to have survived the succession of raids that plagued the city in the 19th century. The *sim* ("sim," main chapel) is regarded as the finest example of the Louang Phrabang style of architecture.

The name Xieng Thong means "The Golden City." It also means "flame tree." On the wall of the rear *sim*, there is a glass mosaic representation of the *thong* ("thong"), or "tree of life." Mosaic decoration is a recent art form in Laos. Two *hor song phra* ("hor-son-PHRA"), or red side chapels, in the spacious compound of Wat Xieng Thong are covered in colored mosaics depicting local village and court life.

Wat Xieng Thong is considered by many to be the most beautiful *wat* in Laos. The buildings embody all the elegance and refinement of Lao religious architecture. The many-tiered roof is one of its most outstanding features. Several roofs overlap each other in a complex and graceful design that swoops almost to the ground. The walls, cross beams, and pillars of the main sanctuary are covered with ornate, gold-stenciled designs. The interior contains more examples of Lao art with gold and bronze Buddhas, embroidered tapestries, and finely carved wooden columns.

The complex at Wat Xieng Thong occupies a superb location overlooking the Mekong. A flight of steps leads directly from the river to the temple compound. In former times this was the main gateway to the city.

LAOTIAN LOOMS

The most common way for Lao women to express themselves creatively is through the weaving of their highly complex and refined textiles.

Lao women weavers are among the finest in Southeast Asia. Textiles are very important to all Tai societies. In Laos the continued popularity of the national dress for women has helped to keep alive an art that has all but vanished elsewhere.

In traditional Lao society, an ability to weave was a prerequisite for marriage. Even now, especially among the hill tribes, it is said that the best way to a man's heart, for a woman, is through her weaving. A woman who is known to be a deft weaver accrues more status than an average weaver.

Looms are often located among the piles that support the house, as this is a cool and shady place to work. Cotton and silk are carded and spun by hand. There is only one cotton harvest a year in Laos. Silk can be harvested four times a year. Silk weavers must feed the worms with mulberry leaves.

The French introduced chemical dyes to Laos. Since the revolution, there has been a revival in the use of natural dyes. These take longer to obtain but, in the eyes of experts, produce much richer and more saturated colors. The origins of dyes are varied. Red, for example, comes from breadfruit and raintrees; indigo from the indigo plant; black from pounded ebony seeds; and yellow from turmeric roots.

Buddhist and animist symbols often appear as traditional motifs in Lao textiles. Other common themes include flowers, hooks, diamonds, *nagas*, casuarina trees, and abstract figures of peacocks, elephants, geese, and dragons. Many of the old techniques and designs have been lost because of war and population displacement among tribes that were the leading exponents of weaving traditions. It is vital that old skills are renewed now, before they are lost forever.

This carved door at Wat Ong Teu is a good example of Lao design.

WOOD CARVING

The Lao have long excelled at wood carving and engraving. Sophisticated craftsmen have been producing decorative religious art for centuries. Large scrolled teak panels on the sides of temples relate scenes from the *Ramayana* or local myths.

The wooden doors and window shutters of temples are usually decorated with elaborate foliage and figures that fill the surface in crowded, though harmonious, patterns. These are often painted in red and gilded. The gables of temple roofs are often made of richly decorated, carved panels in wood and stucco. The edges of the roof are curved upward in order to catch evil spirits.

Many distinctive Buddha statues are made of wood, and fine examples can be seen in the temples of Vientiane and Louang Phrabang. An ornate royal funerary chariot at Wat Xieng Thong is made from carved and gilded wood. The prow of the chariot is shaped into the form of a five-headed *naga*.

High quality wood carvings and sculptures can also be found on the doors, shutters, and gables of recently renovated or reconstructed temples, proving that the art is still very much alive in Laos.

KHMER RUINS

The combination of high ground and water guaranteed that Phu Pasak, near Cham Pasak in southern Laos, would be a sacred place. The priests of Chenla, the civilization that preceded the Khmer, built shrines to the mountain gods and water spirits here. A temple in the form of a *lingam* existed here as early as the sixth and seventh centuries.

Wat Phu, the country's great Khmer temple, was built in the 10th century as a shrine to the Hindu deity Shiva. Archeologists believe that there may have been a road directly connecting Wat Phu with Angkor, 60 miles (97 km) away, in Cambodia.

The main sanctuary at Wat Phu is typically Khmer in design.

Well-preserved reliefs of Hindu gods and goddesses still decorate the temple's portals and ruined facades. Wat Phu was later converted into a Buddhist temple. The mountain behind the temple and its sacred spring have been the focus of worship and meditation by *rishi* ("ree-SHEE," religious hermits) since the 11th century.

Boun Wat Phu, a three-day Buddhist festival, is held at the temple on the day of the full moon of the third lunar month. The festival, which has its origins in the spirit cults of the south, was originally held to appease the guardian *phi* of Wat Phu, and human sacrifices were conducted. Today, this has been replaced with a buffalo sacrifice. The festival is one of the largest in Laos. Pilgrims arrive from all over the south of Laos and from neighboring districts of Thailand. The water tanks at Wat Phu are used for boat racing, and there are music and dance performances, fireworks, elephant races, and buffalo fights. Buddhist, as well as animist rituals incorporating elements of Hinduism, are practiced side by side.

WAT MAI

Along with Wat Xieng Thong, Wat Mai, or the "new monastery," is a treasure of Lao architecture. The temple, with a distinctive five-tiered red roof, took over 70 years to complete. The ceiling of the veranda, containing lotus blossom designs and scenes from the Buddha's life, has one of the best preserved murals of its kind in Laos.

The most striking feature of Wat Mai is the extraordinary golden bas-relief that runs along the facade. This tells the story of the Phravet, one of the last incarnations of the Buddha. It is set in a rural background depicting scenes from village life that are clearly Lao. A closer look even reveals small depictions of Louang Phrabang landmarks like That Chomsi and Wat Xieng Thong. The episodes read like a text, from left to right. A long beam above the frieze, carved in red and gold relief, depicts scenes from the *Ramayana.*

Relating the story of the Phravet, this sumptuous, wooden gilded mural is stretched like a panel at the entrance to Wat Mai.

LEISURE

THE PURSUIT OF LEISURE, in the Western sense of the word, is a concept that is only possible to apply to the wealthier or more fashion conscious elements in Lao cities. Few people are familiar with sports and pastimes like tennis, golf, computer or video games, or the idea say, of taking the car out on the weekend just for the pleasure of a drive.

For most Lao, the notion of developing a hobby or setting aside time for planned leisure activities are unfamiliar approaches to pleasure. The Lao are noted for being a relaxed and easy-going people. The pace of life and work, the general absence of urgency, is reflected in their temperament. The Lao do not have to be told to slow down and relax. The habit is inbred.

Above: **A Lao boy readies his homemade kite for flight.**

Opposite: **Two children enjoy swinging.**

Festivals, temple fairs, and ceremonies connected with birth, ordination, marriage, even death, are important highlights for the average Lao.

Festivals are important to the Lao as they provide the chance for family gatherings. Hill tribes often visit Lao cities at this time to participate in the festivities or to sell their wares to the lowland Lao. There is rarely spare money for holidays or excursions at other times, however. Pleasure is derived from the simple, enduring things in life.

Although more people own radios and cassette players than ever before, only one in every thousand Lao possesses a television set. Years of war and deprivation have denied the Lao the more contrived pleasures taken for granted elsewhere, but have obliged them to also maintain a traditional way of life that continues relatively unchanged, especially in rural areas. The art of conversation has not died out and people still enjoy the pleasure of each other's company. Leisure activities revolve, as they always have, around the pleasures of family life, the community, and the pagoda.

A man strums his guitar, while his friends play a form of checkers with bottle caps.

CITY PASTIMES

Vientiane, with its proximity to Thailand and its growing foreign community, provides the country's most diverse range of leisure activities. Window shopping in the capital's minimarts or new malls has not yet replaced passing the time of day with friends at the open markets, but other Western-style pleasures are having an impact on city life that is beginning to be felt at many levels.

Film is a universal pleasure and going to the movies is a popular pastime with the Lao. The country has no film industry of its own. Most films are dubbed into Lao from Indian and Chinese. Thai films are usually shown in the original. Very few Lao ever go to restaurants, but for those who can afford it, bars and beer gardens are popular places for socializing. These are often set in gardens or on the banks of rivers. For the people of Vientiane, a trip out to one of the cafés, bars, or stalls that have sprung up around the Friendship Bridge has become a popular excursion. Young people are more inclined, though, to spend their time motorbiking around town, listening to Thai rock music, or attending one of Vientiane's nightly discos.

For most Lao, a good harvest, convivial company, and simple pleasures like a walk at sunset through the village or along the Mekong, are the time-honored rewards for toiling in field, shop, or government office.

98

SPORTS AND GAMES

Part of the communist ideology of the post-1975 era was to develop a healthy and vigorous nation through sports. Most Lao cities have a sports stadium. Some of these have been built at the expense of other civil amenities such as good roads. Sports stadiums also serve, however, as places for concerts, National Day celebrations, and for political rallies. In cities like Vientiane, soccer teams regularly work out in the national stadium or compete with rival teams on Saturdays.

Practicing *takraw*, a game popular with many Southeast Asians. *Takraw* is a competition sport at the biennial Southeast Asia Games.

Another popular pastime is *takraw* ("TAHK-raw"), a traditional game played with a hollow cane ball. Two teams compete over a net as in volleyball. The players must keep the ball in the air for as long as possible using only their feet, heels, shoulders, and elbows. A skillful team may be able to keep several balls in the air at the same time. *Takraw* is also played in Thailand, Burma, and Malaysia. In former times the game received royal patronage. These days the game is experiencing a popular revival.

Other popular games include snooker, the French ball game *boules* ("BOO-wl"), and *ti-khi* ("tee-KEE"), a form of hockey played with a curved stick and a ball made from bamboo. Lao-style boxing is a form of martial art. Some of the poses in Lao boxing and other martial arts can be found on the carved steles of ancient Lao temples. The troops of Fa Ngum, the king who first unified the country, are said to have found the discipline useful in battle. Both feet and fists are used in this sport, which resembles a mixture of boxing and karate.

Lao boxing was banned under the French, but is now enjoying a revival thanks to the efforts of the government-sponsored Lao Sports Association.

Before the revolution, Lao orchestras were far larger and more formal than they are now. Many of these were disbanded because of their strong associations with the royal family. These days, with greater tolerance and more freedom of movement around the country, many orchestras are re-forming.

A FEAST OF DANCE AND MUSIC

The Lao have a strong and natural feeling for music. Lao musicians depend largely on their memories and improvisational skills. There are very few formal, written compositions. Vocal music is especially popular in Laos, and songs have been passed down from generation to generation. Early traveling minstrels were influenced by the folklore of India. Songs that have survived are often about love and heroic adventures. They may also be prophesies or songs of prayer.

Typical Lao music is the folk music of the people. The most popular instrument is the *khene* ("ken"), a kind of harmonica or hand organ made from varying lengths of bamboo tubes. Another common wind instrument is the *khuy* ("KOO"), a type of bamboo flute. Two-stringed violins and various percussion instruments are also important. The *khong vong* ("ker-

A musician adds to the gaiety at the That Luang Festival.

100

ONG VON") is a horseshoe-shaped instrument consisting of 16 small bronze gongs that are struck with wooden mallets. Another common instrument is the *nang nat* ("ner-ANG nat"), a small xylophone. These two instruments are almost always included in *seb noi* ("zeb NO-ee") orchestras, which are used in religious processions or at the end of vocal recitals.

Many of the ethnic minorities also have strong musical traditions. Many Khamu tribes, for example, have their own orchestras with clarinets, flutes, xylophones, and single-stringed violins. For the Khamu, gongs are by far the most important instrument. When someone is ill, deafening music is played to drive out or influence evil spirits.

Where there is music, there is also dance. Classical Lao dance has its origins in India. Styles were probably imported from the Cambodian royal court in the 14th century. There are also Burmese and Thai influences in Lao dance. Scenes from the *Ramayana* are sometimes performed in temple compounds. There is usually little or no stage scenery, but the sumptuous costumes and colored and lacquered masks more than make up for the absence of sets.

Young urban Lao seem to prefer to dance to the sounds of Western and Thai pop and rock music in the capital's discos. But even here a touch of tradition prevails. No evening is quite complete without at least one *lamvong* ("lam-VON"), a traditional Lao folk dance in which two circles are formed, with women on the inside. The *lamvong* is also performed at festivals, weddings, and parties.

For young men in some Lao minorities like the Hmong, the tradition of serenading girls they wish to marry in the form of a musical dialogue remains an important custom. To the accompaniment of a khene, or some other instrument, the boy will tell the girl in flattering terms why he has chosen her. The girl will question him and a dialogue will develop.

FESTIVALS

THE LAO ARE A FESTIVE PEOPLE, a fact attested to by the number and wealth of national and local festivals held throughout the year. The word *boun* ("boon") means festival in Lao. *Het boun* ("HET-boon") signifies "merit making," so *boun*, to the Lao way of thinking, are opportunities for both self-improvement through religious observance and the pursuit of earthly pleasures at one and the same time.

The Lao are happy not only to celebrate their own festivals but those of other groups and cultures as well. The New Year is celebrated four times a year—first the international New Year in January; the Chinese and Vietnamese (*Tet*) New Year in January/February; the Lao Buddhist New Year, which falls in April; and finally, the Hmong New Year in December.

Opposite: **Devotees put the finishing touches to a sand stupa during the Lao New Year celebrations.**

Below: **Monks join in at a That Luang Festival parade.**

THE LAO CALENDAR

The Western Gregorian calendar is used in Laos for all government and business matters, but many people, especially in rural areas, still employ the traditional lunar calendar. The Lao Buddhist calendar is based on the movements of the sun and moon. Accordingly, the New Year is reckoned to begin in December, but the Lao choose to celebrate the New Year in April, which is considered a more auspicious month. The Lao calendar is a combination of the old Thai-Khmer and Sino-Vietnamese ones, in which each year is named after a different animal. During the Lao New Year celebrations, paper pennants bearing images of the respective animal symbols are sold. Because the Lao Buddhist year follows the lunar calendar, the timing of many of the festivals varies from year to year.

Trance sword dancers draw an audience at a Lao festival.

MAJOR FESTIVALS

While there are many small annual *boun* centered on local pagodas, there are several major regional celebrations, like the Wat Phu festival in Cham Pasak in the south. The four most important festivals in Laos are considered to be the New Year (*Pi Mai*), the Rocket Festival (*Boun Bang Fay*), the Water Festival (*Boun Lay Heua Pay*), and the That Luang Festival (*Boun That Luang*). The following list also includes other main religious and secular events on the Lao calendar.

JANUARY: *Boun Pha Vet* Held to celebrate King Vessanthara's reincarnation as a Buddha.

JANUARY/FEBRUARY: Chinese and Vietnamese (*Tet*) New Year A time for dances, processions, and fireworks.

APRIL Lao New Year (*Pi Mai*) The preferred date for the Lao New Year.

In May, Labor Day—an event honoring workers the world over—is celebrated in Vientiane.

Colorfully dressed dancers perform in the That Luang Festival.

In October, Awk Phansa *celebrates the end of the Buddhist Lent. Parties are held and boat races take place on the Mekong River.*

MAY: *Visakha Puja* This festival celebrates the birth, enlightenment, and death of the Buddha.

MAY: The Rocket Festival (*Boun Bang Fay*) A Buddhist rain-making festival.

JULY: *Khao Phansa* The beginning of the Buddhist Lent. A time for religious retreats and fasting.

AUGUST/SEPTEMBER: *Haw Khao Padap Din* A festival where the living pay their respects to the dead. Many cremations are held at this time.

NOVEMBER: That Luang Festival A colorful event focusing on the country's most important temple.

DECEMBER: Lao National Day A national holiday to celebrate the 1975 revolution.

THE PI MAI

Few festivals evoke the life and customs of a people better than the Lao New Year, or *Pi Mai*. The *Pi Mai* is known in Laos as the Fifth Month Festival.

In deciding to delay the beginning of the official year by several months, the Lao *horas* ("or-AH," astrologers) placed the New Year under more favorable conditions. The astrological signs at this time of year are believed to point to light and prosperity. The period also anticipates the end of the hot season and the coming of the life-giving rains.

Before the festival begins, each house is carefully cleaned and swept to banish evil spirits, and many temples and homes receive a fresh coat of paint.

A beauty queen passes the former royal palace in Louang Phrabang during a *Pi Mai* procession. Louang Phrabang is generally acknowledged to be the best place to see the festival. Many of the original elements of the event, long since discarded in other regions, remain unchanged here.

A line of women make their way along Louang Phrabang's main street—the best place to view the *Pi Mai* procession.

The festival is an occasion for the Lao to dress up in their best and visit temples. The Lao pray for a good crop and pay homage to the city's most important Buddha statues. It is the monks' task to ritually cleanse Buddha images with holy water. Water is a strong symbol of purification. Monks and anyone who happens to be passing by in the street are doused with pails of water.

Votive mounds in the shape of miniature stupas are constructed from sand in the compounds of temples or along the banks of the Mekong River. The *Pi Mai* is a serious occasion, but not a solemn one. During the day and evenings, the city is alive with parades, beauty contests, musical and dance recitals, dramas, and fairs.

The Lao remain, at heart, a deeply conservative and traditional people. During the *Pi Mai*, young Lao visit their families and superiors to pay their respects. Kneeling humbly before their elders, they pour scented water over their hands and ask for their blessings and expressions of good fortune for the coming year.

BACI CEREMONY

The *baci* ceremony is unique to Tai races and central to Lao culture. The ritual is believed to predate Buddhism. *Baci* are held to celebrate special events and occasions like marriage, birth, welcoming a guest, and homecomings.

They are also held during festivals and private parties. In Laos, novice monks are given a *baci* before they enter the *wat*, mothers are honored with one after they have recovered from giving birth, and visiting officials often receive a *baci*. The ceremony is also dedicated to the sick in the hope of a cure.

Conducting a *baci*, the most important of all Lao spiritual ceremonies.

Many Lao festivals have much in common with those in other Southeast Asian countries, particularly Thailand. What makes Lao festivals unique is that they have retained many of the original elements that have been lost or rejected elsewhere. Less commercialized than the cultural events of many of their neighbors, and more elemental and closer to their animist roots, Lao festivals represent the closest link to many of the pre-Buddhist rites and practices of the region.

The Lao believe that the body is protected by a total of 32 spirits called *kwan* ("KWA-ang"). To enjoy perfect health and balance, all 32 *kwan* must be present. The departure of even one brings with it sickness and even the possibility of death.

The aim of the *baci* is to generate goodwill and hospitality, but the *baci* is also intended to restore balance and harmony to the individual and his or her community. The *baci* ceremony summons the *kwan* back to the body from wherever they may have roamed.

Baci are usually conducted by a respected elder, sometimes in the presence of a monk. Central to the ceremony is an arrangement of flowers, white cotton strings, banana leaves, and candles called a *phakwan* ("PAK-wang"). As guests join hands in an attitude of prayer, the person conducting the ritual chants in a mixture of Lao and Pali, invoking both Buddhist and animist deities and spirits and calling for the *kwan* to return.

White threads are taken from the *phakwan* tree and, with blessings and good wishes, tied around the wrists of guests. The threads should not be removed for at least three days. A meal is served after the ceremony. This is often followed by the *lamvong*, the national dance.

Anyone who is lucky enough to attend a *baci* cannot fail to recognize the warmth and sincerity of this ancient ceremony and its importance as a social and family bond. For the Lao, the *baci* is a unique way of confirming the value of life.

WHITE EQUALS HARMONY

In Laos, the color white is a symbol of peace, harmony, good fortune, and human warmth and community. The cotton threads used in the *baci* ceremony are always white.

THE ROCKET FESTIVAL

Like the *baci* ceremony, the *Boun Bang Fay*, or Rocket Festival, is a good example of the Lao propensity to mix Buddhism and animism. *Bang* ("BA-an") means "bamboo pipe," and *fay* ("fey"), "fire." The festival is traditionally held on the full moon day of the sixth month of the lunar calendar.

The official purpose of the festival is to commemorate the life and achievements of the Buddha. Pilgrimage and merit making are an important part of the events. A more earthy side to the festival, harking back to ancient fertility rites, is connected with the rockets themselves. These are fired into the sky in the symbolic hope of releasing the rains.

The rockets, which are covered in tinfoil and colorful streamers, are made of bamboo and may be as long as 6 feet (2 m). The rockets are carried through the streets to the accompaniment of drums, *khene* playing, and song. The rocket that soars the highest will bring the most prestige to its makers. In former times the rockets were made exclusively by temples. Today they are made by villages, government departments, schools, and trade union groups as well.

A celebrant at the Rocket Festival.

For visitors, the festival is a good chance to enjoy Lao music and dance and performances of *maw lum* ("moor LOOM"), a traditional folk musical that is both bawdy and comical. For rural Lao, the *Boun Bang Fay* is the last chance for high spirits before the hard work in the rice fields begins in earnest.

FOOD

LAO FOOD IS OFTEN COMPARED to Thai cuisine, but there are several ways in which it differs. In common with many of their neighbors, rice is the main staple of the Lao. Dishes are distinguished by the use of spices like ginger, tamarind, lemon grass, and several types of hot chili peppers. A typical Lao dish is a mixture of hot and sweet flavors, moderated by herbs. Because the country has no access to the sea, fish comes fresh from the Mekong and other rivers. One feature of Lao cooking that sets it apart is the way it mixes fish, meat, and herbs in the same dish. Fermented fish (*pa dek*, "pah DEK") and fish sauce (*nam pa*, "nahm PAH"), are also vital staples of the Lao diet. Food is usually prepared on a stove fired by wood or charcoal.

Opposite: **A food vendor prepares a typical Lao snack.**

Left: **An elegant Lao meal served in a Louang Phrabang restaurant.**

FOOD

An important feature of most Lao homes is the kitchen garden. These contain vegetables such as onions, yams, cucumbers, salad greens, eggplants, beans, spinach, and shallots. Condiments like citronella, hot peppers, and ginger may also be grown. Each house normally has its own fruit trees as well. Lao villagers grow bananas, coconuts, mangoes, avocados, lychees, and durians. Home products are a vital supplement to food bought in the open market. Food also plays an important role in the religious practices of the Lao, as anyone who has attended a *baci* ceremony or witnessed monks on their morning alms rounds will know.

A selection of green vegetables and condiments at a Lao market.

BASKETS OF RICE

Rice is highly esteemed in Laos. The Lao are especially partial to glutinous rice (*khao nyao*, "kah-OH nya-o"), although nonglutinous rice (*khao chao,* "kah-OH cha-o") and rice vermicelli (*khao poon,* "kah-OH pewn") are also popular. Family members may eat from a communal bowl or have their own individual baskets. Sticky rice is eaten with the fingers. Rice is rolled into a tight ball and then used as an eating utensil to push and scoop up other ingredients on the plate, or to dip into sauces.

Rice is a versatile staple; it also forms the basis of various desserts and sweets. Rice is mixed with taro, coconut milk, and water-lily roots to make desserts. *Khao tom* ("kah-OH tom") consists of rice stuffed with bananas and then steamed in a banana leaf. Another popular dessert, *tom nam hua bua* ("tom nahm WHOO-er boo-er"), is made by mixing coconut milk and lotus flowers.

Rice is a powerful, life-affirming symbol throughout Asia. In Laos, sticky rice is often pressed onto Buddha statues and the walls of private homes as offerings to the resident spirit. Women are strongly associated with rice in Laos. In many remote villages, legend holds that the rice goddess sacrificed her body in a fire, the ashes helping to produce a bumper crop for the village. In some Phuan villages, the bones of female ancestors are kept in a stupa in the middle of the family's rice fields.

Glutinous rice—a staple of the Lao.

115

POPULAR DISHES

A green papaya salad vendor.

In addition to freshwater fish, pork, chicken, water buffalo, and duck form the main ingredients of many popular dishes. Game such as deer, quail, wild chicken, and small birds are also eaten when they are available. The traditional ceremonial dish of the Lao and the closest thing to a national dish is called *lap* ("lap"). The word means "luck." *Lap* is a party dish often served on special occasions or to honored guests. Often compared to steak tartar or Mexican *cerviche* ("ser-VEECH"), *lap* is made by mixing finely minced beef, venison, or if these two are not available, water buffalo with chopped mint and lemon juice. There is also a fish version of *lap*.

At the other end of Lao cuisine are inexpensive dishes served in markets or at street stalls. One of the most popular is *tam maak hung* ("taam MAK hoong"), a vegetarian salad. This is made by pounding fermented lettuce leaves, green papaya, lime juice, chilies, garlic, and whatever else comes to hand, in a big mortar. Thai-style curries are also popular. These dishes are made hot with the fiery addition of red chilies, but cooled down with the use of slightly sweet coconut milk. The Lao also enjoy Chinese food. The most common dish is *foe* ("fow"), a rice-noodle soup. *Foe* is usually served with a side plate of salad vegetables like lettuce, mint, and bamboo shoots, which can be added to the broth. *Foe* is a popular snack and breakfast dish. Soup of one kind or other accompanies most main meals and is always served in the middle or end, never the beginning.

FRENCH LEGACIES

Many of the old French buildings in Laos may be crumbling, but France's food legacy is as strong as ever. French cuisine can be easily sampled in the restaurants of Vientiane and Louang Phrabang. Dishes like frog's legs and *fillet mignon* ("fee-LEH ming-yong"), a steak dish, remain popular with Lao who can afford such luxuries. French bread, also called French sticks or *baguettes* ("bah-GET"), form the basis of a popular Lao breakfast. These are sold fresh at the morning markets and at bakeries. The Lao tend to dip their *baguettes* into hot milky coffee or to eat them with fried eggs or fish sauce, or as a sandwich with a Lao-style pâté filling.

French *croissant* ("cru-AH-son") and chocolate bread (*pain au chocolat*, "pan o SHO-co-la") are eaten in street cafés with cups of strong Lao coffee. Visitors to Vientiane are often surprised to find bottles of old wines like Bordeaux and Bergerac proudly carried up from the cellars of French restaurants.

French bread is a popular item in the morning. The Lao often buy their breakfast *baguettes* stuffed with Lao-style pâté.

Eating with one's hand is a custom common not just in Laos, but also many other Asian countries.

MANNERS AT THE LAO TABLE

Lao family meals seem like relaxed and informal events, but there are certain customs and manners to be observed. Unlike Western countries where people sit around a raised table, the Lao are more likely to squat on the floor around one or more circular bamboo tables. Instead of having a succession of courses served one after the other, most of the food will be laid out on the table in several dishes at the beginning of the meal. The family or their guests help themselves, eating whatever they like in no particular order.

There are certain ideas and attitudes connected to food and its consumption that foreigners may not always be aware of. One of these is the Lao concept of *piep* ("pyee-EP"). This can be roughly translated as status, dignity, or prestige. In terms of Lao meals, this means that parents, for example, being the elders and therefore the most senior ranking members of the family, always take the first mouthful. Other members follow according to age. From this point onward everyone is free to eat whatever takes their fancy, but no one should help themselves before an older member of the family has first tried a dish, or at the same time as someone else. Guests should not continue eating after everyone else has finished. It is the custom in Laos to always leave something on the plate when you have finished. If a guest does not do this, the host will lose her *piep*, as the implication will be that she did not provide enough food and the guest is still hungry.

The Lao are meticulously clean and have the habit of washing their hands not only before, but also after a meal.

An eye-catching array of river fish from the Mekong.

FLAVORED WITH HERBS

Various kinds of herbs play an important part in Lao cooking. Lao forests, rivers, and even the ditches of rice fields provide a wealth of edible plants. Herbs are used to flavor dishes, but also as a balance to the use of strong ingredients such as garlic and hot chilies.

Most herbs are gathered in the wild, but some kitchen gardens may have a patch for growing ingredients like cinnamon, mint, and coriander leaf. For poor rural families who are rarely able to enjoy meat, freshly-caught fish prepared with aromatic herbs is a delicious and healthy alternative.

DRINKS

The Lao enjoy a mixture of natural drinks like coconut milk, and their own characteristic beverages like *lau-lao* ("LA-oo-lao"), a fermented rice wine. Coconut milk is often used as the base for other fruit juices or mixed with them. *Lau-lao* is made from fermented glutinous, or sticky, rice. White *lau-lao* is the most common and is sometimes drunk with a twist of lime or even with Pepsi, which is now bottled in Laos. *Fanthong* ("fahn-TONG"), a red *lau-lao*, is fermented with herbs. Rural families often make a version of rice liquor for their own consumption. It is the custom at parties, festivals, and other social gatherings for several people at one time to drink *lau-lao* from clay jugs using long straws. A brewery makes beer, available in bottled form or as draft beer (*bia sot,* "bee-ER sot").

Lao coffee is excellent. Most of it comes from the fertile Bolovens Plateau in the south of Laos. It is roasted, ground, and filtered for selling, and also served in cafés and restaurants. The Lao generally prefer their coffee thick and sweet and will add sugar and condensed milk to achieve this. Coffee usually comes in a glass and is served with a complimentary glass of *naam sa* ("nam SAH"), a weak Chinese tea. Both black Indian teas and cured or green Chinese teas are common in Laos.

Laos produces a small quantity of black tea, but not enough at this stage to be self-sufficient.

A LAO DESSERT: *NAM VAN MAK KUAY*

Nam van mak kuay ("nam-VAN-may-KWAY"), a popular banana, tapioca, and coconut milk dish, can be sampled in Lao homes and some restaurants. It is not a difficult dessert to make.

12 bananas
4 cups coconut milk (fresh is better than canned)
$1/2$ cup tapioca
1 cup sugar

Peel and cut the bananas into about 30 pieces. Put the bananas, coconut milk, and sugar into a saucepan and bring to a boil. Add the tapioca and simmer everything for about 20 minutes. The Lao usually serve this dessert while it is hot, but it is also delicious if kept in a refrigerator and served cool.

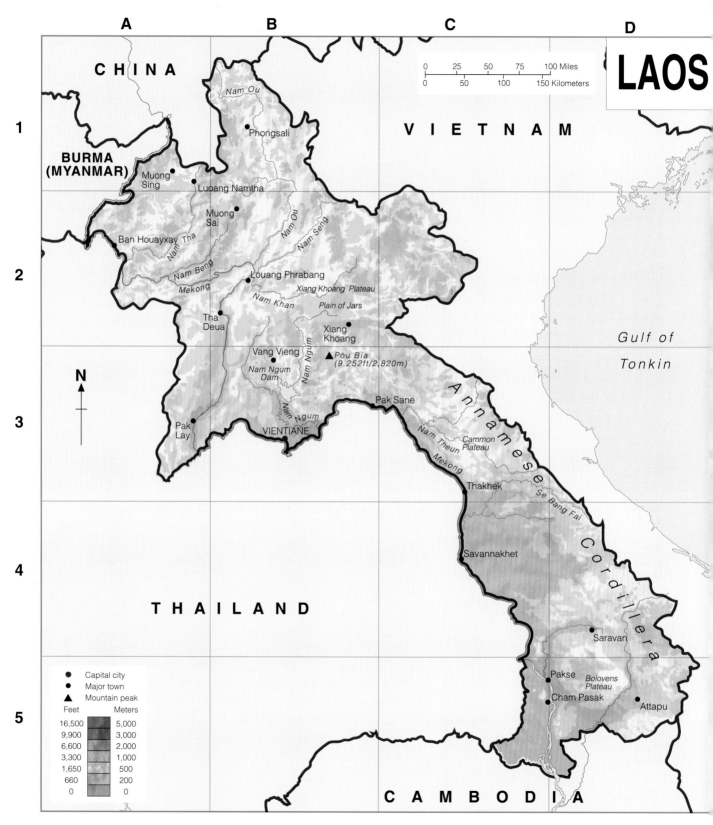

LAOS

CHINA

VIETNAM

BURMA (MYANMAR)

Nam Ou

Phongsali

Muong Sing

Luoang Namtha

Muong Sai

Ban Houayxay

Nam Tha

Nam Beng

Mekong

Nam Ou

Nam Seng

Louang Phrabang

Xiang Khoang Plateau

Nam Khan

Plain of Jars

Tha Deua

Xiang Khoang

Vang Vieng

Nam Ngum Dam

Nam Ngum

▲ Pou Bia (9,252ft/2,820m)

Pak Sane

Nam Ngum

VIENTIANE

Pak Lay

THAILAND

Gulf of Tonkin

Annamese Cordillera

Nam Theun

Cammon Plateau

Mekong

Thakhek

Se Bang Fai

Savannakhet

Saravan

Pakse

Bolovens Plateau

Cham Pasak

Attapu

CAMBODIA

N

| | 0 | 25 | 50 | 75 | 100 Miles |
| 0 | | 50 | 100 | | 150 Kilometers |

● Capital city
● Major town
▲ Mountain peak

Feet	Meters
16,500	5,000
9,900	3,000
6,600	2,000
3,300	1,000
1,650	500
660	200
0	0

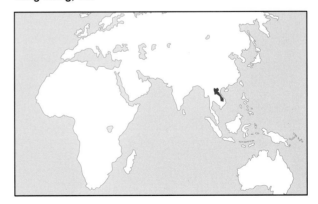

QUICK NOTES

AREA
91,430 square miles
(236,800 square km)

POPULATION
4.5 million (1996 estimate)

CAPITAL
Vientiane

OFFICIAL NAME
Lao People's Democratic Republic

MAJOR LANGUAGES
Lao (official language)
French
numerous tribal languages

HIGHEST POINT
Pou Bia (9,252 feet / 2,820 meters)

MAJOR LAKE
Nam Ngum Dam

MAJOR RELIGION
Theravada Buddhism

MAJOR RIVERS
Mekong, Nam Ou, Nam Ngum, Nam Theun,
Nam Khan

CLIMATE
Tropical, with rainy season between May and
October

MAJOR CITIES
Savannakhet, Pakse, Louang Phrabang, Cham
Pasak

NATIONAL FLAG
Three horizontal bands—a narrow red band at
the top and bottom and one central blue with
a white circle set in the center

CURRENCY
Kip
100 at = 1 kip
US$1 = 900 kip

MAIN EXPORTS
Electricity, timber, garments

MAJOR IMPORTS
Oil and petroleum products, machinery, motor
vehicles, food products, medicines

POLITICAL LEADERS
Fa Ngum, king from 1353–73
Samsenthai, king from 1373–1416
Setthathirat, king from 1548–71
Souligna Vongsa, king from 1637–94
Chao Anou, king of Vieng Chan from 1803–29
Souvanna Phouma, prime minister from 1951–
54, 1956–58, 1960, and 1962–75
Kaysone Phomvihan, prime minister from 1975-
91 and president from 1991–92

ANNIVERSARY
National Day (December 2)

GLOSSARY

baci ("BAH-see")
Ritual held to celebrate special occasions like marriage, birth, and homecomings.

jataka ("jah-TAK-er")
Incarnations or lives.

kampi ("kem-PI")
Lao manuscripts, usually engraved on palm leaves and threaded together with cord.

khene ("ken")
Hand organ made from varying lengths of bamboo tubes.

khong vong ("ker-ONG VON")
Horseshoe-shaped musical instrument made up of 16 small bronze gongs that are struck with wooden mallets.

khuy ("KOO")
A type of bamboo flute.

lamvong ("lam-VON")
Traditional folk dance where two circles are formed, with women on the inside.

lap ("lap")
Ceremonial dish served on special occasions or to honored guests. Made from finely minced beef and venison, with chopped mint and lemon juice. There is also a fish version of *lap*.

lau-lao ("LA-oo-lao")
Fermented rice wine.

mudra ("moo-DRAH")
Attitude, or the way Buddha images are represented.

naga ("NAR-ger")
Mythical water serpent that resembles a cobra.

nam pa ("nahm PAH")
Fish sauce popular in Lao cooking.

nang nat ("ner-ANG nat")
Small xylophone.

nirvana ("ner-VAH-na")
State of nothingness in which a Buddhist is finally free from suffering.

paa beuk ("PAH buk")
Giant Mekong catfish—the world's largest freshwater fish.

pa dek ("pah DEK")
Fermented fish.

pha biang ("PAH bee-ang")
Silk shawl worn by Lao Lum women on special occasions.

pha sin ("PAH sing")
Embroidered, wrap-around skirts favored by Lao Lum women.

phi ("PEE")
Guardian spirit.

samsara ("sum-SA-ra")
Cycle of existence and rebirth in Buddhism.

takraw ("TAHK-raw")
Traditional game played with hollow cane ball.

wat ("what")
Pagoda.

BIBLIOGRAPHY

Cheeseman, Patricia. *Costume and Culture.* Thailand: Studio Naenna Co. Ltd., 1990.

Hamilton, Wanda. *Favorite Stories From Laos* and *More Favorite Stories From Laos.* Singapore: Heinemann Asia, 1990.

Hoskins, John and Hopkins, Allen W. *The Mekong: A River and its People.* Bangkok: Post Publishing Co., 1991

Kaignavongsa, Xay and Fincher, Hugh. *Legends of the Lao.* Geodata Systems, 1993.

Zickgraf, Ralph. *Places and Peoples of the World: Laos.* New York: Chelsea House, 1990.

INDEX

INDEX

INDEX

WITHDRAWN

PICTURE CREDITS
David Simson: 1, 4, 5, 15, 23, 25, 35, 36, 42, 43, 58, 61, 76, 77, 83, 86, 91 (top), 98, 119
Stephen Mansfield: 6, 10, 13, 14, 19, 20, 21, 24, 27, 28, 33, 39, 40, 41, 45, 46, 47, 48, 49, 50, 55, 57, 66, 67, 71, 74, 78, 80, 84, 85, 87, 88, 89, 90, 91 (bottom), 92, 93, 94, 95, 99, 102, 104, 105, 107, 108, 109, 111, 113, 114, 115, 117, 120
Trip Photo Library: 7, 32, 100, 103, 106, 116
Hutchison: 9, 30, 34, 56, 62, 63, 73
Life File Photo Library: 11, 17
Axiom Photographic Agency: 3, 12, 26, 37, 38, 52, 53, 54, 60, 65, 68, 69, 79, 82, 96, 97, 112, 118
Crescent Press Agency: 18, 22, 29, 44, 51, 59, 64, 70, 75, 123
Camera Press: 30